DIY
TIPS

exclusive edition for
SCOTLAND*on*SUNDAY

Welcome to this indispensable guide to DIY, compiled for our readers. It's the perfect partner to Scotland on Sunday's atHome magazine. Every week atHome is packed with tips on homes and interiors, and features hundreds of properties for sale. Let us inspire you every weekend with

*at*Home in SCOTLAND*on*SUNDAY

Lynn O'Rourke, Editor, atHome

HarperCollins Publishers
Westerhill Road, Glasgow G64 2QT
www.collins.co.uk

This edition has been exclusively produced for Scotland on Sunday

ISBN 0 00 776966 0

Printed and bound in Great Britain by Clays Ltd, St Ives plc

Contents

Preventive Home Maintenance   1

The best way to reduce home-repair costs and headaches is to perform preventative tasks on a regular basis. If you inspect your home regularly and keep everything in working condition, you'll cut down on repairs and nip emerging problems in the bud. Use this schedule to stay on top of home maintenance.

Once a month

- Clear leaves and other debris from the path in front of your home.
- Scrub off any algae or moss from the path.
- Test the batteries in your smoke and carbon monoxide detectors.
- Pour a tablespoon full of baking soda down all drains, followed shortly afterward by a cup of vinegar. Let it stand overnight, then flush with hot water.
- Check fire extinguishers to see that they are still fully charged.

Every three months

- Check for cracks in any masonry or stucco on the outside of your home. Seal cracks immediately.
- Check washing machine and dishwasher areas for leaks.
- Clean the filter in the cooker hood.
- Make sure attic vents are open to allow air to escape.
- Drain an electric water heater.

Every six months

- Scrub off any mildew on the exterior of your home.
- Check for water and air leaks in the attic, basement and garage.
- Check the sealant in baths, showers and sinks, and replace it if necessary.
- Check for wood decay.
- Check that the TV aerial/satellite dish is secure.
- Look for any signs of rodent activity.
- Nail down any loose tiles or siding.
- Touch up the paint on the exterior of the house.

Once a year

- Hire someone to inspect your chimney and clean it if necessary.
- Clean out gutters and drainpipes; clear any debris from the roof.
- Inspect the roof for damage.
- Check the seals on windows and doors, and weather-strip if needed.
- Have someone service your heating (and cooling) systems.
- Replace batteries in smoke and carbon monoxide detectors.
- Inspect flooring for wear; refinish or replace if needed.

Maintaining the windows in your home is relatively painless and can save you money on heating, cooling and repair work later on.

⊙ Steps

Maintaining Wood-Frame Windows

1 Start with a visual inspection of the window-panes and the putty that holds the glass in place. Cracked panes and missing putty allow drafts. Replace broken panes or repair the putty (see 3 "Replace a Broken Window-Pane").

2 Look at the paintwork. If it is badly chipped, cracked or chalky to the touch, you'll need to paint the exterior woodwork. A poor paint job allows moisture to penetrate the wood, causing rot and swelling – which in turn causes more paint damage.

3 Inspect where the window casing meets the wall. Use a high-quality paintable latex sealant to fill any gaps or cracks between the window frame and the siding or brick.

4 Make sure that the windows seal tightly when closed. If they are loose, you may need to add weather stripping around the window channels.

Maintaining Metal- or Vinyl-Frame Windows

1 Start with a visual inspection of the window and frames. Rubber seals hold the glass in place. If the seals deteriorate over time, you'll have an air or water leak. The window sash will have to be removed from the unit and taken to a glass-repair shop to have the rubber replaced. You may need to call a professional to remove the window.

2 Check for cracked or broken glass, which should also be replaced by professionals at a glass shop.

3 Look for moisture between panes of glass if you have double-glazed windows. Moisture indicates that the seal between the panes has been penetrated. The space between the panes is usually filled with a gas to help provide insulation; if the seal is broken, the insulation value of the window is less effective.

4 Check around the window casing where it meets the wall; fill any gaps with a paintable latex sealant.

5 Make sure that any weather stripping is in good condition – you can find it seated in a groove in the window frame. Remove a short section of it from the window to take with you to the repair shop to find the right replacement. Remember to take measurements so that you get enough to do all the repairs needed.

✱ Tip

Window putty now comes in a tube that fits a sealant gun. The tip is designed to form beads of putty as you work.

⚠ Warnings

When working with broken glass, wear leather gloves and eye protection.

If your house is two or more stories tall, work carefully on ladders.

Things You'll Need

☐ latex sealant and sealant gun ☐ weather stripping

Replace a Broken Window-Pane   3

Do you have windows that are letting in more air than they should? With a little patience and care you can repair a broken window-pane – it's easier than you might think.

◉ Steps

1 Remove the old glass carefully, wearing gloves and safety goggles. Using a chisel, chip out the old putty around the window and carefully remove the glazing brads (small metal tacks used to anchor the glass in place under the putty, also known as sprigs), so you can take out the glass. You may need to soften the putty with a heat gun or even a hair dryer on a high heat setting.

2 Measure the opening, then subtract 0.3 to 0.5 cm ($1/8$ to $3/16$ inch) from the vertical and horizontal measurements. You don't want the glass to be jammed tightly in the opening.

3 Purchase new glass with the appropriate dimensions. Any glass shop and many DIY shops can cut glass to the size you need.

4 Set your new glass in place, and use at least two glazing brads on each side – more if the opening is larger than about 30 cm (12 in) square. Be careful that you don't press too hard against the glass, or you may break it.

5 Work the putty against the glass and the window frame. Smooth it down with a putty knife or a glazing knife, which looks like a putty knife with a bent end.

6 Let the window set for 24 hours before opening it.

7 Paint the putty to protect it, following the directions the putty came with. Some manufacturers suggest waiting for several days or even longer before painting.

✱ Tip

Large window-panes, or broken or cracked window-panes in metal or vinyl frames, should be left to the pros.

⚠ Warning

Be careful with broken glass, and dispose of it properly.

Things You'll Need

☐ gloves ☐ safety goggles ☐ small chisel ☐ heat gun or hair dryer

☐ replacement glass ☐ glazing brads ☐ window putty

☐ putty knife or glazing knife ☐ paint

Use a Sealant Gun   4

Using a sealant gun is the easiest way to seal against air and water. Use sealant to fill cracks between wood trim and your walls, inside the house and outside.

⊙ Steps

1 Clean the area to be sealed, removing dirt, loose paint and old sealant. Be sure the area is dry before you begin.

2 Load a tube of sealant into a sealant gun, making sure it's well seated at both ends.

3 Use a craft knife to cut the tip of the spout. Cut off as little as possible, taking into consideration the size of the "bead" of sealant you need. Some people like to cut the spout at an angle, while others cut it straight; it doesn't make much difference.

4 Hold the gun at a slight angle. If you're filling a crack, insert the spout if you can; otherwise, run it at the surface.

5 Pull away from the bead slightly as you squeeze out the sealant, rather than push into it, which can be very messy. Use just enough sealant to do the job. (Experiment in an unexposed area. You may find that you'll need less of a bead than you think.)

6 Use your finger to gently press the sealant into the corner or crack.

7 Use a damp towel or rag to clean off most of the excess sealant, then use a dry one to clean off the rest.

✳ Tips

There are many types of sealant available, including silicone, acrylic and latex. Silicone sealant is probably the longest-lasting, but does not take paint well.

Keep a bowl of water at hand. Dip your finger in the water before running it down the bead of sealant.

Things You'll Need

❏ sealant and sealant gun ❏ craft knife ❏ nail or awl ❏ towels or rags

5 Re-Grout and Re-Seal Ceramic Tiles

Is the grouting on your tiles badly stained or cracked? You can have it looking like new in no time.

⊙ Steps

1 Buy a mildew-resistant grout – make sure it's the same colour as your existing grout. Some grouts are pre-mixed; for others, just follow the instructions on the box. You'll also need grout sealer.

2 Prise out old grout with a craft knife. Work carefully to avoid chipping or dislodging tiles. It's a good idea to wear safety goggles for this job.

3 Vacuum or brush dust and dirt from grout lines.

4 Work the grout into joints with a grout float. If you are only repairing a small area, use your finger. Wipe excess grout from the joint with a damp sponge, smoothing the grout to match existing joints. Clean any grout from the tops of the tiles with the sponge. Rinse your sponge often to speed the cleaning process.

5   Allow the grout to dry (this usually takes several hours at least, but overnight may be best).

6   Brush grout sealer onto the new dry grout. Sealing grout prevents it from absorbing water.

✳ Tip

If grout lines have cracked in wet areas, water may have seeped through to the plaster beneath. Allow this to dry thoroughly before re-grouting.

Things You'll Need

☐ grout ☐ grout sealer ☐ craft knife ☐ vacuum cleaner or dust brush
☐ grout float ☐ sponge ☐ brush

Choose the Right Adhesive for a Job   6

Different glues are needed for different tasks; making the wrong choice may result in disaster.

◉ Steps

1   Read the labels. Make sure that the brand you choose is compatible with your purpose.

2   Consider the work surface. Is it porous or smooth? Wood, plaster, paper and cloth are porous; glass, metal, ceramic and plastic are not. Cyanoacrylate ("superglue") and white glue adhere to smooth, non-porous surfaces; hot glue and carpenter's (wood) glue are better for porous surfaces. Contact cement is suitable for both porous and non-porous work surfaces.

3   Decide how quickly you want the adhesive to dry. Superglue bonds instantly; hot glue is quick; water-based contact cement will stick immediately and should be dry within 30 minutes; white and carpenter's (wood) glues take a few hours; silicone sealant requires about 24 hours to cure; epoxies (heat-solidifying resins) vary.

4   Determine whether it needs to be water and/or heat resistant. Two-part epoxy, superglue, water-based contact cement and silicone sealant are resistant to both. Hot glue doesn't hold up well under extreme heat, but is waterproof. Carpenter's glue holds up under moisture and heat, whereas white glue doesn't fare well when exposed to either.

5   Think about cleaning. Silicone sealant, superglue and two-part epoxy can be cleaned up with acetone – which is flammable and toxic. Water-based contact cement, new water-based silicone sealers, carpenter's glues and white glues can be cleaned up with water.

✳ Tip

Latex-based products are nonflammable and far less toxic than solvent-based ones.

⚠ Warning

Always read all warning labels, and glue in well-ventilated areas.

You can repair or replace vinyl sheet flooring and vinyl tiles with excellent results if you know the proper technique.

⊙ Steps

1 Measure the damaged area.

2 Find a DIY store or floor-covering store that sells the pattern of vinyl flooring you need. Purchase enough sheeting or tile squares to repair the damaged area. (It's always a good idea to keep any scraps for future repairs.)

3 Use a sharp craft knife to cut a piece of new vinyl flooring that is larger than the damaged area if you're repairing sheet vinyl flooring. Use a straightedge to keep the blade vertical. Replace whole squares if you're using standard-sized tiles.

4 Line up the pattern of the new piece with the pattern along the edges of the damaged area.

5 Tape the replacement piece of vinyl over the damaged area with masking tape. (Make sure the new piece is secure and will not slip when cutting.)

6 Use a sharp craft knife to cut through both layers of vinyl. Cut an area just larger than the damaged spot. (This way the hole and replacement piece will be the same size.)

7 Remove both pieces of vinyl. Heat the old vinyl with a hair dryer to soften the adhesive before prying it up.

8 Clean debris and old adhesive from the floor with a putty knife. You can soften the old adhesive with a heat gun or hair dryer. Use a broom or vacuum cleaner for final cleaning.

9 Apply adhesive to the floor with a notched trowel or putty knife.

10 Press the new patch firmly in place starting at the centre and working towards the edges to get all the air bubbles out from under the patch.

11 Wipe excess glue from the edges with a damp sponge.

12 Roll the patch firmly with a rolling pin or hand roller. Wipe the edges again to remove any excess glue.

13 Let the adhesive dry well before allowing heavy traffic back in the repaired area.

✱ Tip

The cleaner the floor under the patch, the smoother the finished job will be. Raised areas will wear faster than the rest of the floor.

⚠ Warnings

Some adhesives can give off potentially harmful vapours, so always provide proper ventilation in your work area.

Always make sure to cut away from your body when cutting vinyl flooring.

Things You'll Need

☐ measuring tape ☐ replacement vinyl flooring ☐ craft knife ☐ masking tape

☐ putty knife ☐ heat gun or hair dryer (optional) ☐ adhesive

☐ notched trowel (optional) ☐ sponge ☐ rolling pin or hand roller

Repair a Leaky Gutter   8

You can fix minor gutter leaks with roofing cement. Leaks in the drainpipe – often caused by leaky joints – require resealing.

⊙ Steps

Repairing Leaks in Gutter Railings

1   Clean the leaking area with a wire brush and water.
2   Dry the area and rub with coarse sandpaper.
3   Cover the hole with plastic roofing cement. Spread the cement at least 5 to 8 cm (2 to 3 in) around the hole.
4   Cover with a piece of flashing (sheet metal) if you're dealing with a large hole; press the flashing into the cement and feather the edges of the cement to hold the flashing in place.

Repairing Leaks in Drainpipes

1   Remove the leaking portion of the drainpipe.
2   Clean old sealant or adhesive from the joint with a wire brush.
3   Replace rubber gaskets if you're dealing with vinyl or PVC gutters.
4   Apply a bead of silicone sealant on one joint and then put the gutter back together.
5   Re-attach the gutter with new fasteners or connectors if needed.

Things You'll Need

☐ wire brush ☐ coarse sandpaper ☐ plastic roofing cement ☐ flashing
☐ rubber gaskets ☐ silicone sealant ☐ gutter fasteners or connectors

Repair Wallpaper   9

Torn or damaged wallpaper can be repaired if you have extra wallpaper that matches the pattern. Here's how to make and apply a patch.

⊙ Steps

1   With a craft knife, cut a piece of wallpaper a few inches larger than the damaged section.
2   Place it over the damaged section and hold it in place with "safety" masking tape, making sure that you match the pattern.
3   Use a sharp razor blade to trace the area to be removed, cutting right through both pieces of wallpaper at the same time. Try to make your cuts follow the pattern as best you can. (If possible, align your repairs along a seam.)
4   Carefully remove the top piece of paper and set it aside.
5   Use the razor to lightly score the wallpaper to be removed and apply water to loosen the adhesive (see 19 "Remove Wallpaper").
6   Use a putty knife to remove what you can't lift off with your fingers.
7   Clean or sand the area underneath the paper until it's smooth; use

spackling compound to fill any dents. Apply primer (sizing) if you're down to a raw surface on the wall.

8 Apply wall-covering adhesive to the new wallpaper and place it on the wall.

9 Wipe away any adhesive on the surface with a damp sponge, then use a seam roller (see 20 "Hang Wallpaper") to press down the edges of the patch. Wipe the paper clean again.

✳ Tip

Repair a small tear by brushing on some wallpaper adhesive (or even white glue) and pressing the wallpaper back down. Repair a wrinkle or blister by slitting it with a razor and treating it as you would a tear.

Things You'll Need

☐ craft knife ☐ replacement wallpaper ☐ "safety" masking tape

☐ sharp razor blade ☐ putty knife ☐ sandpaper ☐ seam roller

☐ spackling compound or primer ☐ wall-covering adhesive ☐ sponge

---

10 | Prepare a Room for Painting

It's all in the preparation. Take the time – probably more than you actual spend painting – to get the best results.

⊙ Steps

1 Remove what furniture you can; move what's left into the centre of the room and cover with dust sheets. Use removable "safety" masking tape around mouldings, doors and windows, and dust sheets to protect floors and furnishings.

2 Cover the smoke detector with a plastic bag and turn off heating while sanding or painting.

3 Sand or scrape loose and flaky paint with sandpaper and paint scrapers – down to bare surfaces if necessary.

4 Using a putty knife, fill all nail and screw holes using "plastic wood" or all-purpose filler; fill larger cracks with sealant. On woodwork, use epoxy filler (like that used on car bodies). Whatever you use, sand it down until it matches the area around it.

5 Wash all surfaces with sugar soap or a detergent solution to remove grease and dirt.

6 Rinse everything well with water to remove the sugar soap or detergent. Allow surfaces to dry thoroughly, and then dust and vacuum as needed.

7 Turn off the power to the room, then remove the cover plates from all electrical fixtures, outlets and switches. Place small pieces of masking tape over switch handles and sockets to protect them from paint. It's safest to leave the power off as you paint the room – if you decide to turn the power back on, work carefully around electrical areas.

8 Loosen or remove cover plates from all the light fixtures; cover what remains with plastic bags. Remember not to turn on the lights – melting plastic can smell terrible. Paint during the day to get maximum lighting in the room, or use an extension cable to bring in a light source from another room.

9 Remove heating vent covers.

✳ Tip

Old blankets and duvet covers make excellent furniture covers when decorating.

⚠ Warning

If your home was built before 1980, it may contain lead paint. This is especially dangerous to children and pregnant women. Look on the Defra web pages for further information (www.defra.gov.uk/environment/chemicals/lead).

Things You'll Need

☐ dust sheets ☐ "safety" masking tape ☐ plastic bags ☐ sandpaper

☐ paint scraper ☐ plastic wood/all-purpose filler ☐ putty knife

☐ sealant and sealant gun ☐ epoxy filler ☐ sugar soap or detergent

Paint a Room   11

To paint a room, start with the ceiling and then paint the walls. Finish with the trim.

⊙ Steps

1 Prepare the walls and ceiling (see 10 "Prepare a Room for Painting"). Use a stain-blocking primer to cover any dark mark you can't remove (stains, knots, ink, dark paint); otherwise, that area will bleed through. Never paint on wallpaper (see 19 "Remove Wallpaper").

2 Make sure there is adequate ventilation in the room.

3 Plan on three coats: one coat of primer and two coats of finish. Always use primer on patched and unpainted surfaces; raw surfaces suck up paint like a sponge – or even reject it altogether.

4 Paint into all the corners with a standard 5- or 8-cm (2- or 3-in) brush. Use the same brush to outline where the ceiling meets the wall (and vice versa) around doors and windows, above the baseboard and around any other trim or detailing – and wherever a roller won't fit.

5 Pour some paint into the roller pan and roll away on the ceiling and then the walls. Pour only a small amount of paint in your roller pan – this will keep the paint from drying out before you can use it.

6 Start rolling before the brushed-on paint has had time to dry, so that the rolled-on paint will blend in rather than become a second coat. Rolling out a "W", about 1 m (37 in) wide, and then filling it in, assures an even application of paint. Get as close into the corners as you can without making a messy paint line.

7 Paint from dry areas into wet. This will help reduce any paint ridges. Feather (thin out) all edges as you go, whether using a brush or a roller; this will also help reduce ridges.

8 Cover cans or buckets when you're not using them. Keep a rag and brush handy to deal with drips, spills and the general messiness of the process. If a drip becomes too dry to spread out, let it dry. Come back later, sand it and paint over it.

✳ Tip

If you have mildew, consider adding a specially designed primer – or other additive – to your paint.

⚠ Warning

If you use anything other than water-based latex paint, never put paint-soaked or cleaner-soaked tools or rags in an enclosed area of any kind – even a metal dustbin with a lid. This is a recipe for spontaneous combustion.

Things You'll Need

- ☐ stain-blocking primer ☐ primer ☐ paint or finish ☐ sandpaper
- ☐ 5- or 8 cm (2- or 3-in) brush ☐ paint roller ☐ roller pan ☐ rags

12 Paint Around Windows

As with all painting jobs, the more preparation you do now, the less work you'll have to do later. And of course the window will look nicer, too.

⦿ Steps

1 Look for loose, flaky paint and remove it with a paint scraper and/or sander – all the way down to the wood if necessary. Sand down the areas you plan to paint.

2 If you're going to paint the outside of the window as well, check the putty between the glass and the frame. This seals the window and holds the glass in place – if it's cracked or crumbling, then you will need to replace it.

3 Check the outside for other areas where water could enter between the window frame and the house – or even within the window itself – and seal as necessary.

4 Remove or tape over all the hardware you can, such as locks, handles, latches or hinges.

5 Put masking tape on the glass next to the surface you're going to paint. It makes cleaning up easier.

6 Use primer if you've exposed any raw surfaces. Choose a primer which is appropriate to your surface – wood or metal require different paints.

7 Follow up with a coat of eggshell or gloss paint. It's durable and easy to clean.

8 Use an angled paintbrush and work from the top down. Paint the window frame first, then the trim on the wall around it. Make sure you don't paint windows shut (see Tips).

9 Scrape off any paint that has strayed onto the glass with a purpose-made razor blade – leave it until the paint has dried at least enough to be tacky. Gently run the blade, edge first, between the painted surface and the glass, then lay it flat (like a spatula) to scrape the rest of the paint off the glass.

✳ Tips

If you have sash windows (windows slide up and down behind each other), paint each window separately, allowing one to dry before painting the other, and leave them open a bit while drying so they don't stick to each other or the frames. Don't paint the vertical grooves on the side where the windows actually slide.

Vinyl-covered windows cannot be painted with anything at all.

Things You'll Need

☐ paint scraper or sander ☐ putty ☐ sealant and sealant gun ☐ razor blade

☐ masking tape ☐ primer ☐ eggshell or gloss paint ☐ angled paintbrush

---

Paint the Exterior of a House   13

This may be the most important painting (and preparation) you do. Paint and preparation vary with the type of surface: wood, stucco, metal, masonry. Check with your DIY store.

◎ Steps

1 Consider the weather: You'll want to avoid extreme temperatures, wind and wet weather. Never paint right after it rains, as surfaces will be too wet. Always try to paint in the shade, as direct sunlight can cause the paint to blister. The temperate conditions of autumn and spring are usually best for painting outside.

2 Repair or replace any damaged surfaces, whether wood, stucco, masonry or metal.

3 Wash all surfaces with TSP (trisodium phosphate) and rinse thoroughly with water. Or use a pressure washer to reduce work (these can be hired easily enough). Make sure that surfaces dry thoroughly.

4 Use sandpaper or a paint scraper to remove any loose, cracked, chipping or blistered paint – down to raw surfaces if necessary. Use a small cloth to catch loose bits of paint and debris. If you decide the exterior needs to be sandblasted, hire a licensed professional.

5 Patch all nail or screw holes, gouges and cracks.

6 Seal such places as seams and corners, above door and window trim, and where trim meets siding – or where any material meets a different kind of material, such as trim over masonry. (Exception: Don't use sealant where siding or tiles overlap, or between tiles.) Always use high-grade exterior sealant. Better-quality sealants (such as silicone) actually bond to surfaces like glue and resist breaking down.

7 Use epoxy filler (the material used for car bodies) to repair more serious problems in woodwork.

8 Cover dark stains – for example, a wood knot, old paint, a wood stain – with a stain-blocking primer. The same goes for mildewed areas; you can find stain primers and additives made especially for mildew.

9 Sand all patched, raw and glossy surfaces; all paints need a slightly roughened surface to stick to. You can also use paint de-glosser on glossy surfaces. Remove sanding dust and debris.

10 Remove or cover all light fixtures, plumbing outlets, electrical covers and house numbers.

11 Remove all screens. You don't want to get paint on them; it's difficult (or impossible) to remove.

12 Place dust covers over everything you don't want to paint, such as plants, paths, cars and your neighbours' property.

13 Apply primer over all raw surfaces. Note that different surfaces – paint, metal, wood, stucco – require different types of primer.

14 Allow the primer to dry, then apply at least two coats of exterior paint. Let each coat dry between applications according to the manufacturer's instructions. Use a brush on all woodwork and a paint roller or spray machine for everything else.

✳ Tip

You can't paint vinyl or plastic. If there's a problem with any of these surfaces, you'll probably have to replace them.

⚠ Warnings

If your home was built before 1980, it may contain lead paint. This is especially dangerous to children and pregnant women. Look on the Defra web pages for further information (www.defra.gov.uk/environment/chemicals/lead).

If you're using anything other than water-based latex, never put paint-soaked or cleaner-soaked tools or rags in an enclosed area of any kind – even a metal dustbin with a lid. This is a recipe for spontaneous combustion.

Things You'll Need

- ☐ sandpaper ☐ paint scraper ☐ sealant and sealant gun ☐ epoxy filler
- ☐ stain-blocking primer ☐ paint de-glosser ☐ cloths ☐ dust covers
- ☐ primer ☐ paintbrushes ☐ exterior paint ☐ paint roller or sprayer

14 Prepare Your Home for Winter

Some of these steps will require professional help – call early, as calendars fill up during the weeks leading up to winter.

⊙ Steps

1 Add a second layer of insulation to your loft. (If your house is relatively new, it is probably already suitably insulated.)

2 Seal around window and door glass and trim, and all exterior trim. Install or replace weather stripping on all doors and windows. Check for cracks around pipes entering or exiting the walls and electrical sockets.

3 Install secondary double-glazing if you have it. Consider purchasing secondary double-glazing if you have older windows that are not made from modern insulated or double-glazed glass.

4 Have your heating system checked by a licensed heating engineer. Most boiler manufacturers recommend at least annual inspections.

5 Check gutters and clean them if necessary. If there is substantial snowfall, clogged gutters can result in the basement flooding when the snow melts.

6 Replace any roof tiles that are missing or damaged.

7   Have your chimneys inspected by a chimney service and, if necessary, cleaned (see 35 "Clean Out a Fireplace and Chimney").

8   Check the foundations for areas where water may puddle.

9   Trim trees away from the house. Have dead trees and branches removed by professional tree surgeons, or do it yourself.

10 Drain and shut off outdoor water taps.

11 Insulate any water pipes that are exposed to freezing cold.

12 Replace the batteries in smoke detectors, and check to make sure these are all in working order.

13 Check fire extinguishers and charge and replace as necessary.

14 Make sure you are stocked with salt, sand, and snow shovels if you live in an area where heavy snow is likely.

Things You'll Need

❑ insulation ❑ sealant ❑ replacement weather stripping

❑ secondary double-glazing ❑ batteries ❑ salt ❑ sand

❑ snow shovels

HOME IMPROVEMENT

Buy Replacement Windows   15

New windows can really improve the look of an older home while also improving energy efficiency.

⊙ Steps

1   Consider which windows you want to replace. Do you want to replace them all or just certain ones?

2   Consider the time of year. In all probability the project will take at least several days, during which time your home may be somewhat exposed to the elements.

3   Contact several window-installing companies.

4   Discuss the various window types the installers offer (wood, PVC, aluminium) and the merits and costs of each. PVC and aluminium windows do not require painting, so they are low-maintenance.

5   Discuss the energy-efficiency options (standard insulated glass, low-e glass and so forth) offered by the window company. Consider low-e and other high-tech energy-saving options in the context of the estimated savings on your heating and cooling bills. Do the expected savings justify the extra cost?

6   Ask the window company for references and check them: Were past customers happy with the work done? Was the work completed in a timely manner? Have they had any problems since the installation? Did the contractor leave the site in a clean and undamaged condition?

7   Select a window company based upon price, window type, references and your impressions.

8   Make sure that the window company offers guarantee(s). Sign a contract for the work. If ordering the windows separately from having them installed, make sure that the installer has signed off on the list to verify that the windows specified are correct.

9   Make sure that the window company is properly insured. Get a valid certificate of insurance from the contractor before you pay any money or before the work begins.

✳ Tips

The two most common types of windows are sash and casement. The former have bottom and top sashes that slide up and down to open or close the window; casement windows open like a door.

⚠ Warning

Your window installer will insist on a substantial deposit. Always try to negotiate the smallest possible up-front payment and a schedule that matches the pace of work and material deliveries.

16 | Decorate a Room So It Seems Bigger

Sleight-of-hand decorating can help to stretch the perceived dimensions of a room. Here are some ways to help a small room look large.

⊙ Steps

1   Open up the room by maximising views of the outdoors or of an adjoining, more spacious room.

2   Keep the walls light in colour, as light colours recede.

3   Provide good illumination, which will enhance the sense of space.

4   Paint mouldings, doors and the like in the same colour as the walls. Strongly contrasting elements chop up the space.

5   If there are too many small ornamental items, put some of them away – it will make the room seem cluttered.

6   Paint the ceiling white. Rooms have a greater sense of space with high ceilings, and white ceilings seem higher than darker ones.

7   Run linear flooring such as wood strips and ceramic tile on the diagonal. This creates the longest straight lines possible in the room, and the eye will follow them.

8   Use the same flooring material throughout the space to unify it and make it seem more expansive.

9   Select oversized ceramic tiles – even in small bathrooms.

10 Use furniture that is scaled appropriately to the room. For example, an oversize sofa will eat up too much space in a small room.

11 Decorate windows simply. Besides being the wrong scale for a small room, show-stopping treatments such as billowing curtains encroach into the space of the room.

Floor-to-ceiling mirrors definitely increase the sense of volume in a room.
Keep in mind, however, that this is a look that comes and goes in popularity.

Select the Best Paint Colour for a Room | 17

Choosing a paint colour can be a little tricky because it may be
dramatically affected by lighting and shadows. Here are some
tips for getting the colour just right.

⊙ Steps

1 Study colour schemes you admire in home-decorating magazines and tear
  out any particularly appealing examples. Take them with you when
  shopping for paint.

2 Remember that colour usually seems more intense on walls than it does
  on a sample card. When it doubt, go a shade or two lighter.

3 Keep in mind that yellow and rosey tones give a room a warm feeling.
  Greens, blues and greys are cooler colours.

4 Avoid snow-white except in ultra-modern, minimalist environments,
  because it will seem too harsh, giving a sterile, operating-room effect. It's
  better to go with a white that contains a hint of peach, beige or pink.

5 Save bold colour schemes for rooms where you don't spend long
  stretches of time, such as bathrooms and dining rooms. You may tire of
  these schemes if they're in the home office, kitchen, living room or other
  areas in which you stay for hours.

6 Take fabric with you if you're matching it. If you don't have a swatch, grab
  a sofa cushion, bedspread or curtain panel, for example.

7 Start small, buying just a litre or so of paint, and then cover a section of
  wall with a paintbrush or roller. Or test the colour on a large piece of
  plywood or wallboard scrap, or on a piece of cardboard; set it against the
  walls in the room as the light changes (including artificial light) and
  evaluate it for a few days.

8 Test a two-tone colour scheme by painting two boards – or painting one
  board in both colours.

9 Repeat the test, tinkering with more pink, less peach or whatever seems
  appropriate, in small cans of paint until you're satisfied. Yes, the cost for
  sampling various paints can add up, but it can prevent the disaster of
  applying, say, three large tins of the wrong colour and being forced to
  repaint.

❋ Tip

If you plan to sell your house soon, stick with mainstream colours. These are
more likely to appeal to prospective buyers.

18 Paint Woodwork

Excellent preparatory work and patience are the key secrets to successfully painting wood surfaces, such as skirting boards and door frames.

⊙ Steps

1 Clean the wood surface thoroughly with a specialised cleaner – one that doesn't leave a film that could interfere with the adhesion of the paint.
2 Let the wood dry.
3 Mask off the area around the woodwork carefully with professional masking tape, pressing down very firmly on the tape edges you intend to paint. Try pressing down the edges with a spoon.
4 Place dust sheets as needed.
5 Have one or more paintbrushes in widths appropriate to the wood you are painting. Purchase a high-quality brush or brushes with the type of bristles appropriate to the product you are using, either oil based or water based.
6 Apply a de-glossing product (liquid-sanding solvent) according to the directions, which will specify a waiting period before applying primer.
7 Apply primer; oil-based primer is best. Note that there's often a window of only 30 to 60 minutes in which primer can be applied successfully over de-glosser.
8 Sand rough areas after priming.
9 Let the primer dry; this may take a day or more.
10 Apply oil- or water-based paint, as desired.
11 Let the paint dry. Oil-based paint usually takes much longer to dry – a day or more – but experts generally feel it gives a more durable finish.
12 Apply the second coat of paint.
13 Let the second coat dry, and remove the masking tape. Oil-based paint should be thoroughly dry before you remove the tape, but some paint experts advise removing tape when water-based paint is still slightly tacky; do what your paint-can directions or paint store advises.

✱ Tips

High-quality paints and brushes will yield better results. Quality brushes provide a more even coat of paint and will last through many paint jobs.

Clean brushes thoroughly. Do not rest brushes with their weight on the bristles – it will deform the bristles and ruin the brushes.

Avoid painting on hot, humid days or immediately following rain to avoid getting bubbles in the paint.

⚠ Warning

When using solvent (oil-based) products, ventilate the work area thoroughly. Don't smoke or have any type of open flame (even a gas water heater) in the area.

Things You'll Need

☐ wood cleaner and rags ☐ masking tape ☐ spoon ☐ dust sheets
☐ paintbrushes ☐ de-glossing product ☐ primer and paint ☐ sandpaper

You won't know how difficult – or easy – removing old wallpaper will be until you try. Here are a few guidelines to help you tackle the job.

⦿ Steps

1 Move furniture away from the walls and cover the floor with dust sheets.

2 Pick a corner or an edge of the wallpaper and try to peel it off using your hands, a putty knife or a wallpaper scraper. Some papers are designed to simply peel off.

3 If the paper doesn't peel off, or if the pattern comes away leaving the backing in place, score the paper lightly using a blade or a wallpaper knife. Be careful not to cut into the plaster underneath.

4 Apply plain water, water mixed with a mild household soap, or a commercial wallpaper remover to the wall using a paint roller, squirt gun or large sponge. Saturate the wall several times if necessary; the paper will absorb the water until the glue begins to loosen.

5 Alternatively, rent or buy a wallpaper steamer. Take care – steamers get very hot.

6 Try again to pull the paper off with your hands. You might still have to use a scraper or putty knife, however.

7 Wash away as much of the glue as possible, until you are down to the original painted or primed wall. You might have to use a heavy-duty scouring pad. Wait until the wall is dry and use sandpaper to sand off what remains of the paper, backing or glue.

✱ Tip

If the wallpaper resists your efforts, sand it with very coarse sandpaper.

⚠ Warning

Wallpaper removers can be caustic, creating fumes that can irritate your lungs. Wear gloves, long trousers and sleeves, safety goggles, and a hat. Don't forget to ventilate the room well.

Things You'll Need

☐ dust sheets ☐ putty knife or scraper ☐ razor blade or scoring tool
☐ wallpaper remover ☐ paint roller, squirt gun or sponge ☐ scouring pad
☐ sandpaper

Hang Wallpaper 20

Hanging wallpaper can be an experience you'll never forget. These steps are for plaster walls that have been primed and painted but don't yet have wallpaper on them.

⊙ Steps

Preparing the Walls

1 Look for cracks, nail holes and loose paint or plaster on the walls. Fix them first.

2 Be sure that the walls are clean and dry and that every surface is either painted or primed. You don't want to apply paste to a surface that will just absorb it – the paper might not stick.

3 Remove light switch and socket covers after you've washed the walls.

4 Plan to start papering in a place that is inconspicuous, and remember that your starting point will also be your ending point. (Corners and the areas behind opening doors are good places to start.)

5 Beginning at a doorway or corner, measure a distance that's slightly shorter than the width of your paper. Make a mark at this distance – be sure to make the mark as light as possible so that it won't show through the paper's background.

6 Using a spirit level and a pencil, draw a vertical line from the floor to the ceiling through this mark. If you start at a corner, be sure to use the level, not the corner, as your guide. You will align your paper to this line – again, be sure to make the mark as light as possible.

Hanging the Paper

1 With a craft knife, cut a length of paper that's about 10 cm (4 in) longer than the wall, from ceiling to skirting board. (With a large repeating pattern, you might have to cut the strips longer to make sure the pattern matches up from piece to piece.)

2 Apply paste to the paper (see 21 "Apply Paste to Wallpaper"). Or, if using pre-pasted wallpaper, follow the manufacturer's instructions. (Most professional installers apply paste even to pre-pasted wallpapers, but be aware that this voids some manufacturers' warranties.)

3 Start at the ceiling, aligning the paper with the plumb line you drew on the wall. Allow roughly an extra 5 cm (2 in) to flop against the ceiling, and the same amount to flop below the top of the skirting board.

4 Smooth the paper using a smoothing brush or a plastic smoother (which looks like a wide spatula without the handle). Remove wrinkles by pulling a section of the paper away from the wall until you reach the wrinkle. Smooth out the paper as you lay it back against the wall.

5 Smooth from the middle out, applying enough pressure to push out the bubbles but not pressing so hard that you stretch or tear the paper. If you have an air bubble that just won't budge, poke it with a pin and press down on the paper before the adhesive dries.

6 Trim the paper. Using a wide putty knife, press the paper against the ceiling, skirting board, or corner and trim it with a sharp razor blade. (The putty knife provides a straight edge to guide the blade.)

7 Continue with the next piece, aligning it with the one you just laid down. If a pattern just won't line up between two strips, match it at the most obvious spot – eye level.

8 Roll each seam with a seam roller, but don't press so hard that you squeeze out all the adhesive. Go back 10 or 15 minutes later and roll each seam again.

9   When you reach the end – the place where you started – you'll want to create a clean final seam. Lap the final strip of paper over the first strip and trim both simultaneously.

10 Be sure to wipe any excess adhesive off the paper, ceiling, skirting boards and adjoining strips. Use a wet sponge, following with a dry rag.

✳ Tips

Razor blades get blunt amazingly quickly, so replace them often. You'll be glad you did.

Avoid sliding the paper around. Even if you don't tear it, the paper might stretch.

⚠ Warnings

After removing electrical socket covers, you'll be wallpapering right over exposed electrical connections. Be sure to turn off the electricity to the room before cutting around these fixtures. Water, electricity and metal are a dangerous combination.

Place pieces of tape over the sockets and switches to minimise their exposure to paste and water. But remember, the tape won't in any way protect you if the electricity is still on.

Things You'll Need

☐ cleaning supplies ☐ tape measure ☐ spirit level ☐ pencil ☐ craft knife
☐ wallpaper ☐ wallpaper paste ☐ smoothing brush or plastic smoother
☐ pin ☐ wide putty knife ☐ seam roller

Apply Paste to Wallpaper   21

Pasting wallpaper can be a messy job. Here's how to apply paste well and (relatively) neatly.

◎ Steps

1   Be sure that you have the correct adhesive paste for the job. Some papers, such as vinyl backed or lightweight, require a specific paste.

2   Mix wallpaper paste that comes as a powder in a separate bucket and then pour it into the paste bucket or roller tray you will use for the job. Stir well with a stirring stick to remove all the lumps, but not so well that you put a lot of air into the mix.

3   Pour liquid adhesive directly into a bucket or roller tray.

4   Lay a strip of wallpaper – already cut to size, pattern side down – on a long, flat, dry table (the table won't stay dry for long). Let one end of the paper flop over the edge of the table.

5   Use a paste brush or a paint roller to apply the paste to the half of the paper that remains flat on the table, being sure to cover every inch.

6   Fold the section you just pasted over onto itself, and slide the dry section of the paper onto the table. Apply the paste.

7   Fold the next section onto itself, then fold the two halves against each other, being very careful not to crease the paper. This process is called

"booking". Booking keeps the paper moist, the paste from dribbling onto the floor and the pasted surface clean.

8   Set the paper aside in a clean spot for no more than 5 minutes before hanging it.

9   Keep your workspace clean: As soon as each strip of wallpaper is booked and set aside, use a clean, wet sponge to clean the table – but don't bother to dry the surface. Do this even if you're going to paste several pieces before you hang them; you'll want to get the adhesive off the table before it has dried.

✳ Tips

You're going to get paste on the table, the pattern face of the paper and yourself. Don't be overly concerned – it's water-soluble.

Let the paper set after applying paste. This allows the paper to expand or shrink before you lay it on the wall. It also takes a few minutes for the paste to activate the dry adhesive on pre-pasted wallpapers.

Things You'll Need

☐ wallpaper paste ☐ buckets ☐ roller tray ☐ stirring stick
☐ paste brush or paint roller ☐ sponge

---

22 | Hang a Shelf on a Wall

Adding storage or display space in your home can be a simple matter. Here's how to mount a simple wooden shelf and two brackets to a wall.

⊙ Steps

1   Buy a wooden shelf from a DIY store. Buy two shelf brackets – simple "L" shapes or something more decorative – making sure that the top leg of the bracket is no longer than the shelf is deep.

2   Buy screws if you don't have a supply at home or if they don't come with the brackets (see Tips).

3   Buy rawlplugs of a size corresponding to the screws.

4   Determine where you want the bottom edge of the shelf to sit, then mark the position in pencil, using a spirit level as a guide.

5   Line up the top of each bracket with the pencil line and mark the attachment holes on the wall. Set the bracket aside.

6   Drill the holes to a depth appropriate to the screws. Check the depth of the screwholes by inserting the rawlplugs. They should nestle snugly in the holes.

7   Attach the brackets to the wall by screwing screws into the rawlplugs until they grip firmly. Lay your shelf on top, and screw the bracket into the shelf.

✳ Tip

Choose screws that will be able to go into the wall about 2.5 cm (1 in). Choose shorter screws for mounting the shelf on the bracket, so they won't penetrate the top of the shelf.

Things You'll Need

☐ wooden shelf ☐ shelf brackets ☐ screws ☐ rawlplugs ☐ spirit level
☐ drill

Measure Your Window for Curtains   23

Whether you make your own curtains, buy off the shelf or order
custom made, knowing the correct measurements for your
window is the key.

⊙ Steps

1. Decide what kind of curtains you want.
2. Decide where the curtain rod will go. You'll probably want it positioned about
   15 cm (6 in) above the window frame, but you might want it higher or lower
   (or even – for a dramatic look on a tall, deep window – inside the frame).
3. Decide how much coverage you want. Curtains usually extend about 15
   cm (6 in) above the window frame, 6 to 8 cm (2 to 3 in) on each side, and
   6 to 8 cm (2 to 3 in) on the bottom. Consider how much light you want to
   block out – probably a lot if the window is east-facing and you like to sleep
   in of a morning – and how much privacy you want the curtains to provide.
4. Use a tape measure to measure from the curtain rod to the bottom point,
   and from side to side. Multiply the side-to-side measurement by two to
   allow for generously full curtains.

✱ Tip

Make sure the salesperson understands that these are desired finished
dimensions of your curtains, and NOT the dimensions of your window. (It is
of course helpful if you provide window dimensions as well.)

Buy a New Carpet   24

Whatever your style or budget, you can find a carpet to fit your
needs and tastes.

⊙ Steps

1. Decide which areas of your home you want to carpet.
2. Measure the rooms that you want to carpet.
3. Go to several carpet stores. Try both carpet-only showrooms and general
   DIY stores. Ask about installation costs – unless you plan to lay the carpet
   yourself.
4. Consider the various grades of carpeting available. Are you carpeting a
   high-traffic location or a less frequented area of your home?
5. Consider your long-term needs. Is it worth paying more for a carpet that
   will last ten years instead of five? Do you expect to move or re-decorate
   within that time?
6. Take samples of any carpet you are considering so you can view them with
   your walls and furniture.

7 Expect carpet prices to vary considerably according to quality and style. Typically sold by the square metre, carpeting can cost from under £10 per square metre for basic carpet and upwards of £50 per square metre for luxury carpeting. These figures may not include installation.

8 Make your selection after considering cost, style, colour and durability.

9 Decide what type of underlay you want beneath the carpeting. Often, a certain level of padding will be included in the installation price, and you will have the option to upgrade.

10 Ask the retailer to send someone to your home to measure the area to be carpeted.

11 Clean and empty the room before the installers arrive.

12 Check the carpet to make sure that it is clean and properly installed before accepting an invoice.

✳ Tip

Extra padding is an effective way to improve the feel of less expensive carpeting and is well worth the extra cost.

⚠ Warning

Be extremely careful cutting and measuring carpet if installing it yourself.

25 Strip Wood Furniture

Anyone who's ever found cherry or tiger oak underneath layers of old paint knows that while some pieces may not be worth the effort of stripping, others most certainly are.

⊙ Steps

1 Make sure there's no chance that your piece of furniture is an antique whose value could be destroyed by stripping the finish.

2 Set up your work area in a well-ventilated place with nothing around that could produce flames or sparks.

3 Remove drawer handles and other hardware and place the furniture on a layer of newspaper (or an old sheet). You may want to put some scrap wood or bricks udner it, especially if you're stripping the legs, to prevent it sticking.

4 Paint on a thick layer of stripper. Wear gloves and safety goggles.

5 Allow enough time for the stripper to work. (It usually takes 5 to 10 minutes).

6 Scrape the bubbled paint (or varnish) and stripper off in strips, using a paint and varnish scraper, an old spatula, or a putty knife; use an old toothbrush or cotton swabs for crevices. Take care not to scratch or mar softwood or gouge through thin veneers.

7 Repeat if necessary. Two applications are often required, especially if it's an old piece with several layers of stubborn paint or varnish.

8 Wipe down the piece of furniture with clean rags and white spirit, and allow to dry. Don't skimp on the white spirit – you want the piece to be as clean as possible.

When you're finished, dispose of all brushes and remaining stripper as instructed by the paint stripper's manufacturer.

⚠ Warning

Even the new "safe" strippers are caustic. If any stripper gets on your skin, wash it off immediately with soap and warm water.

Things You'll Need

- ☐ newspapers or old cloth
- ☐ stripper and brush
- ☐ gloves and safety goggles
- ☐ scraper
- ☐ toothbrush or cotton swabs
- ☐ clean rags and white spirit

Paint Wood Furniture · 26

Painting furniture involves sanding, priming and painting. Have the patience to apply that second coat of paint – you'll be rewarded with a better-looking, longer-lasting finish.

⊙ Steps

1 Make sure there's no chance that your piece of furniture is an antique whose value could be destroyed by changing the finish.

2 Set up your work area in a well-ventilated place with nothing around that could produce flames or sparks.

3 Remove drawer handles and other hardware. Place the furniture on a layer of newspaper or a disposable dust cloth.

4 Sand the piece of furniture until smooth using fine-grade sandpaper (or liquid sander). Wear gloves, safety goggles and a dust mask.

5 Remove any residual sawdust with a hand vacuum, brush or barely damp rag – you don't want to wet the wood.

6 Apply a coat of either white brush-on or grey spray-on water-based primer, depending on the size and area of the piece of furniture you intend to cover.

7 Allow the primer to become dry to the touch; this usually takes 1 to 2 hours. (Read the recommended drying time on your can of primer.)

8 If the primer coat looks spotty or thin, apply a second coat and allow it to dry.

9 Sand any rough areas.

10 Add a coat of water-based paint. Brush it on with even strokes, going in the direction of the wood grain. With spray paint, make slow passes with the can 20 to 30 cm (8 to 12 in) from the wood surface. Allow the first coat to dry.

11 Add a second coat and allow it to dry overnight.

✴ Tips

Wash paintbrushes immediately after use. Rinse them under fast-running water until the water runs clear from the bristles.

When using spray paint, cover a wide area with newspaper to protect adjacent surfaces.

⚠ Warning

Always work in a well-ventilated area.

Things You'll Need

☐ newspaper or dust cloth ☐ fine-grade sandpaper or liquid sander

☐ gloves ☐ safety goggles ☐ dust mask ☐ hand vacuum, brush or rag

☐ paintbrushes or spray gun ☐ water-based primer ☐ water-based paint

---

27 Apply Wood Stain

Stains are designed to enhance the natural colour of wood. The key is to put a stain on evenly and to keep your work area free of dust and other contaminants.

⊙ Steps

1 Set out a layer of newspapers to protect the work area.

2 Set the temperature in the room between 22 and 24°C (70 and 75°F). If it's too cold or too hot, the stain's drying time will be affected.

3 Sand the wood smooth and vacuum or brush off debris. Oil-based stains in particular will look patchy if the wood isn't smooth.

4 Wet the wood slightly with a wide, clean paintbrush. This helps the stain spread more evenly.

5 Make sure that you have enough stain on hand for the job. If you have to buy more, it may come from a slightly different colour lot.

6 Apply the stain using a clean rag or paintbrush. Brushes are much more effective for staining ornate carvings, door frames, skirting boards and other irregularly shaped areas. Rags hold more stain and are easier to use on flat surfaces.

7 Use a spray gun to apply quick-drying alcohol-based stains (or dip the object in a stain bath for five minutes if a sprayer is too big or unable to reach fine details).

8 Wipe off excess stain with a paper towel.

9 Let the stain dry and then apply another coat if there are patchy areas.

10 Finish the project with varnish, shellac or wood polish to preserve the stain.

11 Dispose of rags per instructions on the stain can.

✳ Tip

Use the stain liberally. Don't pour it onto the wood's surface, but don't be stingy with it.

⚠ Warning

Be cautious with stains – they can be flammable. Use them in well-ventilated areas, and wear gloves and a face mask when applying them.

Things You'll Need

☐ newspapers ☐ sandpaper ☐ vacuum cleaner or brush
☐ wide paintbrush ☐ rags ☐ spray gun ☐ wood stain ☐ paper towels
☐ varnish, shellac or wood polish

Renovate Second-hand Furniture   28

Second-hand furniture is often inexpensive and can easily be
renovated. Here are some ways to update used furnishings.

⊙ Steps

1 Sand lightly, or use a liquid sanding product, and then paint wooden
pieces (chairs, shelves, tables, sideboards) where the clear-coated finish
has seen better days. Painted "antique" and faux finishes are popular;
chequered and squiggle designs also are fun; or you may want to
embellish that painted piece with decoupage (collage).

2 Disguise a bad tabletop by having a mirror cut to cover the entire table,
edge to edge. This works for dining tables and side tables, too.

3 Or you can hide a bad tabletop with a layer of ceramic tile. Use moulding
or sanded, varnished wood strips at the edges of the tile to fill to the
perimeter of the table.

4 Re-upholster a dining-table chair with a pop-out seat. It's easy: you
remove the old fabric and then cover with new one, using a staple gun to
fasten it on the seat bottom. Make it taut but don't stretch it.

5 Cover up soiled or worn upholstery fabric on a dining chair by sewing a
new chair pad that ties onto the back of the chair. A chair pad with a ruffle
on the front and sides usually hides the old upholstery completely.

6 Camouflage the blemished upholstery on a sofa or easy chair with a throw.
Tuck it down deeply behind the back of the cushions.

7 Cover up the soiled arms of an upholstered chair or sofa by draping a
pretty table runner over each arm.

8 Apply decorative brass-nailhead trim to hide nicked edges on wood
furnishings such as tabletop edges and shelving.

9 Renovate filing cabinets, bookcases or tables by covering them with
textured wallpaper – the type that mimics plaster friezes or pressed-tin
ceilings. You can then paint and glaze the piece. (Aged metallic finishes
look spectacular on some types of furniture.)

10 Renew dull clear-coat finishes – varnishes, lacquer and the like – by
cleaning with white spirit and possibly ultrafine steel wool; then apply a
new coat of finish over the old (test first in an inconspicuous spot). This is
a great way to save a picture frame or tabletop.

11 Revive an old trunk or cedar chest by scrubbing the exterior and lining the
inside with wallpaper or by stapling in a tightly woven fabric, such as a
new bed sheet. A flat braid can hide seams and corner imperfections.

12 Wrap a badly damaged table or nightstand with fabric. The fabric can be
fitted, almost like a slipcover, in a box shape for a rectangular table or
draped over a round table; have glass cut for the top so that a non-
washable fabric won't be easily soiled.

13 Replace ugly, dated drawer pulls and knobs on a classically shaped chest of drawers, sideboard or similar piece.

14 Touch up small nicks and scratches on stained wooden pieces using special crayons (sold at paint and hardware stores) – or even with an eyebrow pencil or shoe polish.

✱ Tip

Altering the finish on any piece of furniture that might be a fine antique could reduce its value tremendously. Have a qualified person examine and appraise the piece for you first.

⚠ Warning

Be especially cautious about upgrading old baby furniture. Crib slats on older furniture may be so far apart that they pose a strangulation hazard for the baby; old painted finishes may contain lead.

29 | Apply Wax to Wood

Wax can make an old finish look new again while protecting the wood underneath. Good waxes contain carnauba and beeswax, and some have a silicone element to add shine.

⊙ Steps

1 Seal new wood with a coat of clear varnish before waxing.

2 Clean old wood along the grain with a mixture of one part linseed oil to three parts white spirit on a piece of fine steel wool. Go over the surface again with white spirit on a rag and let it dry. Make sure that you have adequate ventilation when working with white spirit.

3 Apply liquid wood wax with a soft cloth. Pour wax on the cloth, not directly onto the wood.

4 Use circular motions and cover the entire surface.

5 Wait an hour or so and buff the first coat of wax with a clean, soft cloth.

6 Apply another coat, working with the grain.

7 Buff it again after an hour, and then once more after six or more hours.

8 Dispose of rags soaked with white spirit according to the instructions on the manufacturer's label.

✱ Tip

Wax polish should be used only on indoor woodwork, as it lacks durability.

Things You'll Need

☐ clear varnish ☐ linseed oil ☐ white spirit ☐ steel wool ☐ rags
☐ liquid wood wax ☐ soft cloth

Schedule Housekeeping Tasks   30

Keeping the house clean is an everyday chore, but you don't need to do it all every day. Some tasks you'll want to take care of daily; others you can put off for a week; still others you need to perform only once a year. To keep on top of the work, follow this schedule.

Once a day

- Make beds.
- Pick up clutter.
- Throw dirty clothes in a laundry basket.
- Clean out bath and shower drains.
- Wipe off shower or bath.
- Wash dishes.
- Rinse kitchen sink.
- Empty kitchen rubbish.
- Wipe off kitchen counter.
- Wipe oven top and hobs.
- Sweep floor.

Once a week

- Change bed linens.
- Vacuum carpets.
- Dust furniture.
- Clean shower or bath.
- Clean toilets.
- Throw out spoiled food in fridge.
- Empty all rubbish.
- Disinfect worktops.
- Flush sink disposal unit with cold water.
- Mop floor.

Once a month

- Clean toothbrush and soap holders.
- Clean telephones.
- Clean the undersides of tables and chairs.
- Clean fridge shelves.
- Clean fridge exterior.
- Clean items on kitchen worktop.
- Disinfect rubbish bins.
- Clean oven, including range and backsplash.
- Check for cobwebs on ceilings, and vacuum.

Every three months

- Wash or dry-clean quilts, duvets and bedspreads.
- Launder throw rugs and shower curtains.
- Wash blinds, shades, and curtains.
- Wash windows.
- Wash walls, mouldings and skirting boards.
- Wipe cabinets, woodwork and any smudges off walls.
- Clean fridge coils.
- Defrost freezer.
- Polish silver.

Every six months

- Vacuum and turn mattresses.
- Empty bathroom cabinets and responsibly dispose of outdated medicines.
- Shampoo carpets.
- Wax or polish furniture.
- Empty kitchen cabinets and clean inside; throw away all outdated food.
- Clean tops of kitchen and bathroom cabinets.
- Vacuum behind large appliances.

Once a year

- Empty dresser drawers and vacuum inside.
- Roll up area rugs and vacuum underneath.
- Clean ceiling fixtures.
- Re-seal wood floors.
- Go through all paperwork (bills, statements, notices) and recycle everything you don't need.
- Organise remaining papers in a filing system.

31 | Deep-Clean Your Carpet

For heavily soiled carpets, shampooing is recommended, rather than spot-cleaning. Wet-cleaner machines spray and remove hot detergent solution while cleaning the carpet.

⊙ Steps

1. Purchase or rent a wet-cleaner machine, also known as a steamer, at a hardware or DIY store. When you rent a machine, the necessary cleaning products are usually included or can be purchased at the rental store.
2. Vacuum the floor thoroughly.

3 Spray heavily soiled areas with pre-spray or traffic-lane cleaner. For those really dirty areas, increase the amount of pre-spray used instead of increasing the amount of carpet shampoo.

4 Fill the machine's hose or reservoir with hot tap water.

5 Use the machine and carpet shampoo according to the steamer manufacturer's instructions.

6 Maximise the amount of water removed from the carpet by making a water-extraction pass with the water spray on, and then again with the spray off. Test the carpet with your hand. If your hand comes away with water droplets, extract again with the spray off; if your hand comes away damp and the carpet feels wrung out, you have extracted correctly.

7 Wait overnight for the carpet to dry before walking on it. To help it dry thoroughly, open windows and use fans.

✳ Tips

Special solutions are available to treat pet stains and odours.

To help your cleaning last longer, neutralise detergent residue left on the carpet by steaming with a rinse made up of a few drops of vinegar in a bowl of water.

⚠ Warning

Over-saturating the carpet can cause water to soak through and damage the floor underneath.

Things You'll Need

❑ wet-cleaner machine (steamer) ❑ pre-spray or traffic-lane cleaner
❑ carpet shampoo

Care for Silver   32

Extended exposure to air can tarnish your precious silver. Here's how to keep your silver flatware looking clean and new.

◉ Steps

1 Handling helps keep silver free of tarnish, so use it regularly.

2 Avoid exposing silver for long periods of time to foods such as eggs, mustard and mayonnaise, all of which are high in sulphur, and can corrode silver.

3 Avoid leaving silver on rubber mats to dry – rubber also contains sulphur.

4 Wash and dry silver by hand.

5 Use a soft dish towel when drying silver.

6 Apply silver polish according to label instructions.

7 Rub the polish in thoroughly.

8 Buff the surface of polished silver with a fresh, dry polishing cloth until the silver has a bright sheen.

9 Thoroughly remove the polish from the silver before use; silver polish tastes terrible.

0 If silver is to be stored for a long time, pre-treat it with a tarnish-retardant polish before storing.

✳ Tip

Frequent polishing of silver-coated or -plated items may wear down their silver finish, leaving the base metal exposed. Rather than polishing such items, use them as often as possible and wash them by hand to prevent tarnishing.

Things You'll Need

☐ silver polish ☐ soft dish towel ☐ soft polishing cloths
☐ tarnish-retardant polish

33 Polish Brass and Copper

Taking care of your brass objects and accessories is simple, and you may already have the necessary products.

⊙ Steps

1 Dust brass and copper regularly.

2 Wash in warm, soapy water; rinse and dry.

3 Use a commercial brass or copper cleaner as directed. A combination of toothpaste and Worcestershire sauce also works, although it is not as powerful as a commercial cleaner.

4 Apply with a soft cloth, wipe off, and buff with a clean, dry cloth.

5 Avoid using harsh chemicals, abrasive cleaners or scouring pads.

⚠ Warning

Do not polish lacquered brass or copper items.

Things You'll Need

☐ brass or copper cleaner ☐ soft cloth

34 Care for a Mattress

Your mattress may be hidden under blankets and sheets, but it still needs special attention from time to time. If well cared for, it will last about 10 years.

⊙ Steps

1 Cover your mattress with a cotton mattress pad, which will absorb perspiration and can be removed and washed to keep the mattress clean.

2 Rotate your mattress twice a year, or more often if instructed by the manufacturer. Flip it over completely after the first six months. Then, after another six months, flip it over and turn it so that the head is at the foot of the bed. Some new mattresses don't need turning over. Check with the manufacturer.

3   Use the handles on the sides of the mattress for positioning only – not for carrying. Lifting by the handles can damage your mattress.

4   Air out your mattress each morning by folding back the covers to the bottom of the bed for half an hour before you make it. This will also prevent moisture build-up.

5   Try not to sit on the edge of the bed in the same place every day, because this can lead to sagging.

✳ Tip

Leave the "do not remove" tag attached to the mattress. You will need this for filing warranty claims.

⚠ Warning

Avoid stain damage to your mattress. Many manufacturers void their warranties if there are stains.

Clean Out a Fireplace and Chimney   35

A clean fireplace and chimney is your best defence against a dangerous chimney fire.

◎ Steps

1   Buy a set of chimney rods and brushes at the hardware shop.

2   Change into old clothes and don safety goggles and a dust mask. Lay out a clean dust sheet in front of the fireplace. Cover the fireplace opening with a plastic dust sheet held on with duct tape.

3   Open the fireplace's damper. This is the metal door up inside the fireplace, located just above the firebox; it prevents cold air from entering your home when you don't have a fire burning.

4   Carefully climb up on your roof, taking the rods and brushes with you.

5   Remove the chimney cap – sometimes called a spark arrestor – and check it for weather damage. The purpose of the chimney cap is to keep sparks from escaping your chimney. It also serves to keep out rain, small animals and debris.

6   Assemble the chimney rods and brushes according to the equipment manufacturer's directions.

7   Run the brush down the chimney, using a short up-and-down plunging motion. Some brushes are designed to twist as well.

8   Go back inside the house and use a short chimney brush to clean the flue, which is the pipe that runs between the fireplace and the chimney.

9   Use a vacuum cleaner or small broom and dustpan to remove the cold ashes and creosote from the fireplace and the damper.

10 Brush the floor and walls of the fireplace with a stiff scrubbing brush.

11 Use the brush to clean the creosote built up behind the damper.

12 Reach through the damper with a vacuum hose and vacuum the creosote out of the "smoke shelf", a cavity behind the fireplace.

13 Vacuum up all of the dust and debris.

✸ Tip

Depending on how often you use coal fires, consider hiring a professional to inspect your chimney and fireplace for any possible dangers, and to clean them out. This should cost less than £75.

⚠ Warning

Don't use water to clean the fire brick or cement blocks. It could affect heat retention.

Things You'll Need

- ☐ chimney rods and brushes ☐ dust mask and goggles
- ☐ plastic dust sheets ☐ duct tape ☐ vacuum cleaner
- ☐ stiff scrubbing brush

36 | Clean a Barbecue Grill

To make your cleaning easier, try spraying the grill with a non-stick spray before you barbecue.

⊙ Steps

1 Put on rubber gloves.

2 Remove ash from the collector pan beneath the grill. (Make sure the charcoal is completely cool.)

3 Remove the grill's cooking and charcoal grates from inside the bowl.

4 Coat the bowl of the grill with spray-on oven cleaner.

5 Replace the grates and coat them with spray-on oven cleaner as well.

6 Wait as directed in the oven cleaner's directions.

7 Remove the grates again, and set them on newspaper. Scrub residue off the grates with a rag, steel wool or a wire brush, as needed. (If the grates have a non-stick coating, use a plastic scrubbing pad.)

8 Wipe out the bowl of the grill with wadded newspapers.

9 Use a high-pressure hose to rinse off the bowl and the grates.

10 Dry the grates and put a very light coating of cooking oil on each one.

11 Remove stains from the lid using warm, soapy water and a fine steel wool pad.

⚠ Warning

Avoid using harsh cleansers on any part of your barbecue grill.

Things You'll Need

- ☐ rubber gloves ☐ oven cleaner ☐ newspaper
- ☐ rags, steel wool or wire brush ☐ plastic scrubbing pad ☐ hose
- ☐ cooking oil

Rust is tough, but you can get rid of it on most surfaces. Here's an overview of your options for treating and preventing rust on common objects.

⊙ Steps

1 Put on rubber gloves.
2 Treat the affected material (metal or otherwise) with a rust-removing agent that contains oxalic acid, taking care to follow instructions on the product label.
3 Treat the most severe rust stains (especially in toilet bowls) with a pumice scouring pad along with the rust-removing agent.
4 Prevent indoor metal items from rusting by keeping their surfaces dry, dusting regularly and wiping down occasionally with a damp cloth. Dry immediately after wiping down.
5 Keep outdoor wrought-iron structures rust-free by removing existing rust with a wire brush, some sandpaper or a sandblaster. Then go over bare spots with rust-inhibiting primer and paint the surface with rust-resistant metal paint.

Things You'll Need

☐ rubber gloves ☐ rust remover ☐ pumice scouring pad
☐ wire brush, sandpaper or sand blaster ☐ rust-inhibiting primer
☐ rust-resistant metal paint

PLUMBING

Modern taps usually feature a replaceable interior cartridge that houses the unit's moving parts. Drips and leaks can often be stopped by simply replacing this cartridge.

⊙ Steps

1 Turn off the water at the water-supply valve. This is usually beneath the sink (or in the wall behind the shower assembly – often housed behind a removable panel). If there is no water-supply valve in the same room, turn off the water supply for the entire building.
2 Before taking the taps apart, turn them on full to drain the water from the pipes.
3 Remove the handle from the tap. Most handles are fixed with a screw, which is usually hidden under a decorative cap – depending on the make, this can be unscrewed or prised off with a small screwdriver. Remove the screw, then lift or jiggle the handle off. Put the handle in safe place after its removal.
4 Carefully pull the cartridge out of the fixture using a pair of pliers. (Some

makes of tap may have a lock ring or lock nut that holds the cartridge in place. This must be removed with a screwdriver or pliers before the cartridge can be taken out.)

5 Take the cartridge to a hardware shop and purchase a replacement.

6 Install the new cartridge and reassemble the tap.

7 Turn the water supply back on, keeping an eye out for leaks.

⚠ Warning

When working with chrome or brass fixtures, be sure to protect the surfaces from tool damage using a piece of leather, heavy cloth or duct tape.

Things You'll Need

☐ screwdriver ☐ pliers ☐ replacement water-valve cartridges

39 | Repair a Dripping Showerhead

A constantly dripping showerhead doesn't just waste water, it can also drive you crazy.

⊙ Steps

1 Unscrew the showerhead from the water pipe. This can be done by hand but sometimes requires a monkey wrench or large pair of pliers. The head may be held on with a screw, which you'll have to remove.

2 Look at the screw thread inside the showerhead where it fixes into the pipe. You should find a small washer made of plastic or rubber. Replace it if it looks even a little damaged or brittle.

3 Wrap the showerhead stem with PTFE tape to seal the connection.

4 Remount the showerhead on the stem. Don't screw it on too tightly – hand-tightening should be sufficient.

5 Turn the water on and off. Wait several minutes and check for drips or leaks. If the showerhead is still leaking, you may have problems with the shower's water-control valve and need to call a plumber.

⚠ Warning

When working with chrome or brass fixtures, be sure to protect the surfaces from tool damage using a piece of leather, heavy cloth or duct tape.

Things You'll Need

☐ monkey wrench or large pliers ☐ screwdriver ☐ replacement washers
☐ PTFE tape

40 | Fix a Running Toilet

If your toilet goes through more water than Niagara Falls, the problem is most likely to be the diaphragm of the ball cock or the water tank flap valve.

⊙ Steps

Identifying the Source

1 Remove the lid of the cistern and place it out of the way on the floor.

2 Investigate the ball cock diaphragm. It's a valve attached to the float (which is either a metal or plastic ball on the end of a long rod or a plastic canister that slides up and down a vertical plastic pipe). If you can see water coming from this valve, it may need to be cleaned or replaced.

3 Reach down into the bottom of the tank and press down on the edges of the flap valve (a black or red rubber cone that fits into the tank's hole). If the sound of water running into the bowl stops, you know that the flap valve may be worn and needs to be replaced.

4 Get ready to work. Turn off the water supply to the toilet (this valve is most often found coming out of a wall near the toilet; turn the handle in a clockwise direction). Flush the toilet to drain some of the water and make your work easier.

5 If you need to replace the diaphragm or flap valve, take the old one with you to a hardware or plumbing supply shop to make sure you buy the correct replacement.

Cleaning or Replacing the Ball Cock Diaphragm

1 Snap off the cover of the ball cock and put it out of the way.

2 Remove the screws holding down the top plate of the ball cock – the float-control arm is attached to this and may be spring-loaded. You'll see a rubber diaphragm.

3 Remove the diaphragm carefully, noting which side is up, and check its condition. Sometimes a piece of gravel or rust or a hard-water deposit can get lodged under the diaphragm and cause it to leak, or the diaphragm can simply become worn out with age.

4 Replace the diaphragm or clean it by rinsing it in the tank's water; flush the valve by turning on the water supply for the toilet just enough to get a flow of water for a couple of seconds.

5 Replace the top plate and secure it with its screws.

6 Turn the water supply back on, allowing the tank to fill, and replace the lid.

Replacing the Flap Valve

1 Remove the flap valve. Some have a clamp-type assembly, while others hook to short posts that stick out from the overflow pipe; all attachments are fairly easy to remove by hand.

2 Install a new flap valve.

3 Turn on the water supply and replace the lid.

✳ Tip

If these strategies don't solve the problem, you may need to hire a plumber to disassemble the toilet to look for cracks or a worn connecting gasket.

Things You'll Need

☐ screwdriver ☐ replacement diaphragm ☐ replacement flap valve

41 | Unblock a Sink

If your sink is blocked up, try these simple steps before calling in a plumber.

⊙ Steps

1   Remove the sink strainer or plug from the drain.

2   Fill the sink halfway with water, if it's not already full.

3   Place the plunger over the drain, making sure that the plunger's rubber globe or cup is full of water. Plunge five or six times using careful but forceful strokes.

4   Remove the plunger and give the sink a chance to drain.

5   After the sink is completely unblocked, run hot water down the drain for several minutes.

6   If that doesn't work, remove the trap (or U-bend) or use a plumber's snake.

7   Consider a chemical drain cleaner only as a last resort and follow the manufacturer's directions carefully. Do not mix chemical agents, as dangerous reactions could occur.

8   Call in a plumber for problems you can't resolve on your own.

Things You'll Need

☐ plunger ☐ plumber's snake (optional) ☐ drain cleaner (optional)

42 | Thaw a Frozen Pipe

Frozen pipes can be a huge inconvenience, and may cause water damage if they burst. Here are a few quick cures.

⊙ Steps

1   Turn on the tap nearest the pipe. Don't force it if it's too stiff.

2   Wrap the pipe in a towel and secure it with duct tape.

3   Pour boiling water over the towel. Repeat until the water has thawed and runs through the tap.

4   Alternatively, wrap the pipe in a heating pad or place a heat lamp next to it. If you don't have one of these, a handheld hair dryer or a small electric heater should do the trick.

⚠ Warning

Don't use electrical appliances if there is standing water.

Things You'll Need

☐ duct tape ☐ heating pad, heat lamp, hair dryer

You can stop – or at least slow down – a leak, thus preventing water damage until a plumber can do the full repair. These steps are for a temporary fix, not a long-term cure.

⊙Steps

1 Tighten a threaded joint with a pipe wrench if the leak is there. If that doesn't stop the leak, it may at least slow it down until the joint can be replaced. (Note: Some older plumbing may require brazing – a kind of welding. If the pipe has no threads, or you see signs of welding, leave this job to the professionals.)

2 You may be able to plug a very small hole by inserting the tip of a sharp pencil. Break off the tip in the hole and cover with duct tape, wrapping it in several layers.

3 Alternatively, apply epoxy putty specially formulated for leaks caused by cracks or small holes.

4 Fix larger holes by clamping a piece of hose around the pipe. With a knife, cut a length of hose at least 5 cm (2 in) longer than the hole. (Rubber hose or even an old piece of garden hose will do.) You will also need three hose clamps. Slit the hose lengthwise and fit it around the pipe, then clamp the hose in place using a hose clamp at each end and one in the middle.

5 Catch the spillage with a bucket, or – better still – avoid using the leaky plumbing until proper repairs can be made.

⚠ Warning

Use caution – old joints and pipe can be fragile. Rough treatment may worsen the problem.

Things You'll Need

☐ pipe wrench ☐ pencil ☐ duct tape ☐ epoxy putty ☐ hose
☐ knife ☐ hose clamps

SECURITY

Burglarproof Your Home   44

Having your home burgled is a painful experience. Take these precautions to help prevent thieves getting into your house.

⊙Steps

1 Keep windows closed and doors locked – don't take chances for even a few minutes. Bolt all exterior doors from the inside. Secure sliding glass doors by inserting a broomstick or dowel in the inside track.

2 Consider installing an alarm system or motion-detecting lights.

3 Suggest that someone is at home by using electric timers to turn on the radio and house lights at certain hours. Vary the lights that you turn on.

4 Make sure that outside doors are made of metal or a sturdy wood.

5   Check to ensure that doors fit tightly in their frames. If they don't, install weather-stripping around them.

6   Etch valuables with your name and telephone number (or e-mail address) in visible places. If you don't want to ruin valuables by marking them, photograph them instead. Keep an inventory of your property.

7   Keep jewellery and other valuables in a safe.

8   Consider getting a dog – most will make enough noise to discourage burglars.

9   Leave spare keys with a neighbour rather than hidden outside your house.

10 Keep shrubs and bushes trimmed so that they can't conceal prowlers.

⚠ Warning

If you install an alarm system, learn how to use it properly to avoid false alarms.

45 | Replace a Lock

Replacing an existing lock – whether for security or mechanical reasons – is a relatively easy job. These instructions are for a deadlocking cylinder lock.

⊙ Steps

1   Take the old lock out of the door by using a screwdriver to remove the screws on the inside panel of the lock. Be sure to note how the lock comes apart.

2   Grasp the inside and outside pieces of the lock face.

3   Pull them away from the door.

4   Remove the screws from the lock-mechanism plate, which is on the edge of the door.

5   Measure the diameter of the hole in the door, or take the old lock to the hardware shop or lock shop to ensure that you purchase the proper-size replacement.

6   Place the new locking mechanism in the hole on the edge of the door.

7   Use the screws provided to attach the plate to the door edge.

8   Work the inside and outside halves of the lock cylinder into proper alignment. Secure them to the door with the screws provided.

9   Be sure that the bolt plate on the edge of the door is flush-mounted with the surface of the wood. Sometimes the hole for the plate will need to be enlarged slightly with a wood chisel.

10 Test the lock a few times from both the inside and the outside to ensure that it has been assembled properly.

Things You'll Need

☐ screwdriver ☐ tape measure ☐ replacement lock ☐ wood chisel

46 | Choose a House Alarm System

Alarm systems for the home can be complex and expensive, so it's crucial to determine your security needs before you begin consulting with alarm companies.

⊙ Steps

Conducting Preliminary Research

1. Survey your home and determine how many windows and doors you want to be "switched" or integrated into the system.

2. Determine possible locations for the control panel and keypads. You might find it convenient to place a keypad close to the front door. You might also want a keypad close to the bedrooms. The control panel commands the system, and the keypads allow you to program the system and turn it, or its components, on and off.

3. Determine how far away windows and doors are from the control panel so that you know how far wires will be routed if you choose a wired alarm system or how far a wireless system needs to communicate with sensors. Keep in mind that it is difficult to install a hard-wired security system unless your house is still under construction.

4. Decide whether you want a security system that will be monitored 24 hours a day. The central monitoring station "watches" your home for a monthly fee. A less expensive alternative is a basic sensor system with a dialling accessory that connects the system to your phone lines and dials pre-selected numbers if the house's security is breached.

5. Consider your lifestyle. Does anyone in the family often get up in the middle of the night for a snack? Do you have a large pet that roams the house at night? Such circumstances will influence the type of motion sensor you select and how it is installed. It may also result in frequent trips to the keypad to prevent false alarms.

Choosing the System

1. Consult a reputable home security system advisor.

2. Choose a system with a control panel that can monitor all the zones you have in your home. Each window or door integrated into the system is considered a zone. A basic system is capable of controlling eight zones. However, many panels permit the addition of expansion modules that allow the system to watch up to 32 zones.

3. Determine if the routing of the wires for a hard-wired security system might be too long. With a wired system, you will have to drill holes in walls where wires will have to be routed. If the wire run appears too long to you, choose a wireless system.

4. Make certain that a wireless system can perform up to the distance of the farthest zone.

5. Be certain that the system you choose can accept fire-protection sensors, combustible-gas detectors, thermostatic switches (especially in cold climates) and water detectors. Make sure that panic buttons are or can be included.

6. Choose a system that is user-friendly. Make certain that inputting codes into the keypad is not a complicated process and is one that everyone in the family can learn quickly. You don't want to have to refer to the owner's manual as you input or try to interpret codes.

7. Work the keypad of the system you select to assure yourself that it is easy to use. Encourage all family members to work the keypad so that you will select one that everyone can use comfortably.

✽ Tips

You may want to include some kind of alarm noisemaker. A blast of a siren or alarm bell not only alerts neighbours that an intruder is in your home, but also can scare the trespasser away.

A motion sensor outside the home can provide an early warning and, when used with a noisemaker, can discourage an intruder from entering your home.

GARDENING

47 Care for Your Garden, Season by Season

Your garden follows an annual cycle of growth and dormancy. And you, the gardener, must keep up with this cycle. Use this guide to help remind you of the tasks that need to be completed every spring, summer, autumn and winter. Keep in mind that this is a general guide; adjust the tasks to your local conditions.

Spring

- Sow annuals in containers indoors.
- Transplant seedlings into the garden when any chance of frost damage is past.
- Feed shrubs, trees, climbers and ground cover plants.
- Stake climbing and tall plants if needed.
- Deadhead spring-flowering annuals and perennials.
- Prune shrubs that flower on new growth.
- Prune shrubs that have finished flowering.
- Prune climbers to shape them.
- Lay turf or sow seeds for a lawn.

Summer

- Transplant annuals for summer and autumn flowering.
- Feed fruit-bearing plants.
- Continue to deadhead flowering plants.
- Remove dead branches from evergreens.
- Prune climbers that flower on old wood after flowering.
- Mulch to save water and control weeds.
- Dig up, divide and store spring-flowering bulbs.
- Feed roses after each flush of blooms.
- Prepare soil in areas where you plan to plant in the autumn.
- Keep summer flowers and vegetables constantly moist.

Autumn

- Plant spring-flowering bulbs.
- Plant lettuce and other cool-season vegetables.

- Lay turf or seed for a lawn.
- Plant hardy perennials.
- Net ponds to stop leaves falling in.
- Rake and dispose of fallen leaves and other debris.
- Divide perennials.
- Remove dead and diseased wood from shrubs in late autumn
- Move frost-intolerant container plants to a protected spot.

Winter

- Plant bare-root trees, roses and other shrubs before spring growth starts.
- Protect plants from severe cold with plastic sheeting, hessian or other material.
- Prune dormant fruit trees and soft fruit bushes before spring growth starts.
- Mulch young fruit trees and bushes.
- Sharpen lawn mower blades and shears.
- Prune roses in winter to early spring, depending on climate.
- Start seeds of flowers and vegetables indoors.

Begin a Compost Heap 48

Make the greatest organic matter you can ever add to your soil – start a compost heap. Recycle your garden and kitchen waste and watch nature's most basic process unfold in your garden.

⊙ Steps

1   Start a very basic compost simply by piling up leaves and grass clippings. If you do nothing else, you can dig out compost after about six months of warm weather.

2   For something a little more thought-out, start by finding a good place for your heap – somewhere that is handy for the garden and kitchen, yet not prominently in view.

3   Enclose that compost with a simple frame – loosely roll 2 m (6 ft) of chicken wire to make a ring. Leave three cut ends of wire exposed to secure the ring to itself and stand it up.

4   Build a more permanent compost bin from slatted wood or recycled pallets. Leave it open on one side for access – adding, turning and digging out compost from the bottom – and do not cover the top.

5   Understand the two basic elements that make compost: green (grass clippings, old annuals) and brown (dry leaves, soil) garden debris. Try for a balance of one part green to one to two parts brown, until the mix is damp but not wet.

6   Put a layer of leaves 10 cm (4 in) thick in the bottom of your heap, then 2.5 cm (1 in) of your good garden soil. Next add 5cm (2 in) of grass clippings or old plants, then more brown and green in alternate layers.

turn with a fork one week after building your heap. Begin burying coffee grounds, eggshells and green kitchen waste into the heap and turn it weekly. You'll have compost in about two months.

Make another ring or bin and turn the compost from one into the other to neatly mix it up and aerate the heap for fastest results. (Start another heap after yours has grown to 1 cubic m/1 cubic yd.)

9 Begin digging out compost from the bottom of the heap when you turn it over and cannot recognise the component parts any longer. Dig out shovelfuls of crumbly brown compost to use in your garden, and use the partially composted matter for mulch or to start another heap.

✱ Tips

Healthy compost smells pleasantly earthy – turn it more often and add more dry brown matter if yours smells bad.

Water your compost heap only during extended dry weather, and then only enough to moisten it, not drench the contents.

Many excellent compost bins of varying sizes are available ready-made at different prices.

⚠ Warning

Do not compost animal waste, meats, oils, diseased plants or plants treated with weed killers.

Things You'll Need

☐ garden and kitchen waste ☐ chicken wire or wood ☐ garden fork

49 | Create a Lawn

Create a healthy lawn as a key part of your garden and reap more rewards than beauty alone. It can also be a functional part of the garden, for relaxing or for children to play.

⊙ Steps

1 Choose the right type of grass for your needs. Decide whether you will start with grass seed or turf.

2 Sow grass seed in spring or autumn (or summer if there is a good watering system). Lay turf at any time of year, but not in very dry weather.

3 Test your soil – the simplest way is to test it yourself with a home kit, but you may be able simply to check with neighbours or a nursery that knows local conditions. Find out what nutrients you have and lack, what the pH is, and whether or not you need lime or sulphur. Check also how free-draining the soil is.

4 Improve the soil by spreading 5–8 cm (2–3 in) of organic matter, such as compost or ground bark, over the planting area. Also spread a starter fertiliser, which is usually high in potassium and phosphorous, if it's called for after a soil test.

5 Dig over the soil to incorporate the organic matter to a depth of 15–20 cm (6–8 in). Firm the soil thoroughly to create a level surface.

6   In dry areas or for large high-quality lawns, consider an irrigation sy
    to simplify watering. Place enough sprinklers or hoses and pipes arc
    to irrigate, or have an underground system installed.

7   Smooth the planting area with a the back of a rake.

8   Sow seed or lay turf over the planting area.

9   Keep the area moist until the grass is firmly established (six to eight weeks
    on average).

✳ Tips

Much of the equipment needed to plant a lawn can be borrowed or rented
from your local nursery.

To make raking easier, water the area thoroughly three or four days before
planting.

⚠ Warnings

Keep kids and dogs off the grass until it's at least 4 cm (1½ in) tall and ready for
mowing.

Avoid letting your newly planted lawn dry out. You may need to water more
than once a day for at least a week after planting.

Things You'll Need

☐ grass seed or turf ☐ soil testing kit ☐ organic matter ☐ fertiliser
☐ fork ☐ rake

Plant a Lawn From Seed   50

Planting grass from seed is an inexpensive way to grow a
beautiful new lawn, but you need to prepare the soil carefully and
watch over the sprouting seeds. Here are the basics.

◉ Steps

1   Select the right type of grass seed. The most common mix for a hard-
    wearing surface is perennial ryegrass with red fescue, smooth-stalked
    meadow grass and browntop or highland bent. Other mixtures are
    available for high-quality lawns or shady areas.

2   Measure the area of your new lawn to determine how much seed you'll
    need. Purchase the seed at a local nursery or garden centre. Information
    on the packet will tell you how much to buy.

3   Prepare and level the soil, as described in 49 "Create a Lawn".

4   Set your seed spreader at the appropriate setting and fill it with half the seeds.

5   Walking at a steady pace, sow the seed over the planting area, moving
    back and forth in opposite directions. Repeat the process using the rest
    of the seeds, walking at a 90-degree angle to your original paths. This will
    ensure that the seed is sown evenly.

6   Rake over the area lightly. This will help keep the seeds from drying out.

7   Push a roller over the entire area to make sure the seeds and soil are in
    good contact.

the seedbed thoroughly so the soil is moist to a depth of 15–20 cm
in). Apply the water slowly so that the seeds do not wash away.

ep the seedbed moist (but not soggy) until the seed germinates and the
ew grass is a few centimetres high. In hot weather you may have to water
.more than once a day.

⚡ Tips

Once you have thoroughly watered the seedbed after planting, you only need
to water enough to keep the top 2.5 cm (1 in) moist. Germination will take 5
to 14 days, depending on weather and grass type.

When the grass is 2.5–5 cm (1–2 in) high, you can begin to water less often;
avoid letting the planting area go completely dry.

⚠ Warning

Heavy watering may wash away the seeds, and watering too frequently may
rot the seedlings.

Things You'll Need

☐ grass seed ☐ seed spreader ☐ rake ☐ roller ☐ watering equipment

51　Plant a Lawn From Turf

Planting turf (living green grass) turns a patch of dirt into a
beautiful lawn instantly. Here are the basic steps.

⊙ Steps

1　Select the right type of grass for your area (see 50 "Plant a Lawn from
Seed").

2　Measure the area of your new lawn to determine how much turf you'll
need. Purchase fresh turf at a local nursery or garden centre, or have it
delivered from a local turf farm.

3　Prepare and level the soil, as described in 49 "Create a Lawn." The final
level should be 2.5–5 cm (1–2 in) lower than the final lawn height to
accommodate the thickness of the turf.

4　Pick up the turf or arrange to have it delivered on the day you are ready to
lay it. Inspect the turf carefully to make sure it hasn't dried out. Reject it if
it has dried, curled or cracked edges, or yellowing grass.

5　Start laying the turf along a straight edge, such as a drive or path. To
create a straight edge, stretch a string across the centre of the lawn.

6　Position the turf pieces so the ends butt up tightly against an edge or
previously laid piece. Unroll the turf. Place edges as close as possible,
but don't overlap them.

7　Stagger pieces as you move from row to row (as if you were laying bricks)
so the ends don't all line up.

8　Use an old kitchen knife to cut turf to fit in odd-shaped areas.

9　Fill in any large spaces between pieces of turf with soil.

10　Push a roller over the entire area to make sure that turf and soil are in
good contact and to help level the area, or firm with the back of a rake.

11 Water thoroughly so the soil is moist to a depth of 15–20 cm (6–8 in).

12 Keep the planting bed moist (but not soggy) until the turf roots knit with the soil below. In hot weather, you may have to water more than once a day to prevent turves drying out and shrinking.

✳ Tips

Lay the turf on dry soil to avoid a muddy mess.

When laying turf, kneel on a plank of wood so you don't disturb soil or damage turf, and use kneepads to keep your knees from getting sore.

Laying turf is hard work. Enlist help, and use a wheelbarrow to cart pieces around.

Keep pets and kids off your new lawn by enclosing it with stakes and string.

⚠ Warning

Avoid letting turf dry out. Occasionally sprinkle it with water from a handheld hose, and store pallets of turf in the shade.

Things You'll Need

☐ turf ☐ string ☐ old kitchen knife ☐ roller or rake

Mow, Edge and Trim a Lawn   52

Conscientious mowing, followed by edging and trimming, reduces weeds, thickens turf and improves the lawn's appearance and vitality.

⊙ Steps

Mowing

1 Choose the proper mower for your type of lawn. Cylinder mowers provide a fine finish on a high-quality lawn, while rotary mowers are good for mowing large areas. Hover mowers are ideal for small or awkward areas.

2 Set mower blades to the proper height according to grass type and time of year. Set the blade height by placing the mower on a flat, paved surface. Use a ruler to measure between blades and pavement. Adjust according to the manufacturer's instructions.

3 Mow the lawn when the grass is about a third higher than the recommended mowing height.

4 Leave grass clippings on the lawn, unless the grass has grown very tall between mowings. They will contribute organic matter and nutrients as they break down.

Edging and Trimming

1 Use grass shears around trees, under hedges or in places that are hard to reach.

2 Use a nylon-line trimmer (strimmer) to trim and edge large lawns or to cut grass too tall to mow.

3 Create a neat edge to your lawn by using a half-moon edger (a small semicircular blade) between beds and lawn. Push the blade in with your foot so that it slices off a thin piece of turf, leaving a clean, straight edge of soil between lawn and bed. You can also use this to cut edges on worn pieces of turf, or to cut out and remove turves.

4 If you use a half-moon edger, return slices of soil to the garden beds to break down; chop slightly and bury them under the mulch for a neat, nourishing edge.

5 Use edging shears to trim grass that is overhanging the edge of the lawn.

✸ Tips

Mow more frequently in summer when the grass is growing quickly. When mowing for the first time at the end of winter, give a high cut initially, then lower the blades slightly with each cut. An average guide for the height of cut to aim for is 1–2.5 cm (½–1 in).

Mow at the upper end of the height range during hot weather or periods of drought. Taller grasses have deeper roots and survive heat and drought better than shorter grasses.

⚠ Warning

Wear protective footwear and eye protection and follow manufacturers' safety instructions. Remove young children and pets from the area being mown.

Things You'll Need

☐ lawn mower ☐ grass shears ☐ nylon-line trimmer ☐ half-moon edger
☐ edging shears

53 | Reseed Bare Patches in a Lawn

Whether they're caused by pests, weeds, dog urine or a bad golf swing, those little bare spots in your lawn are easy to repair. The trick is to keep on top of them.

◎ Steps

1 Rake and remove the dead grass and debris from the bare patch.

2 Use a fork or hoe to loosen the soil in the bare area.

3 Incorporate 5–8 cm (2–3 in) of compost into the prepared area.

4 Smooth the area with the back of a rake until the new soil is level with the surrounding area.

5 Seed thickly and evenly (taking care not to overcrowd the seeds or jumble them on top of each other). Incorporate the seeds into the soil gently, using the back of the rake.

6 Cover the seeded area with a thin layer of fine compost or other organic matter to act as a protective mulch.

7 Water gently so you don't wash the seeds away.

8 Protect the area from birds if they are a problem. Insert 30 cm (12 in) long

wooden stakes into the ground surrounding the perimeter of the patch, keeping the stakes 25–30 cm (10–12 in) apart. Tie humming tape or aluminium foil strips to the stakes. This will frighten birds away.

9   Keep the repaired area moist until the seed germinates. Once the new grass is established, resume regular watering.

✻ Tip

If the bare patch is due to a petrol spill or dog urine, flood the area with water to dilute the problem fluid. Other measures may be needed in order to control lawn disease or insects.

Things You'll Need

☐ rake ☐ fork or hoe ☐ compost ☐ grass seeds ☐ wooden stakes
☐ humming tape or aluminium foil

Plant Bulbs in Autumn   54

Spring-flowering bulbs such as daffodils, tulips and hyacinths are generally planted in autumn. Here's how to do it right and ensure a wonderfully colourful spring.

⊙ Steps

1   Select bulb types.

2   Arrange for delivery, or make your purchase, so you can plant in autumn. If you are not going to plant them for a while, store them in a cool, dry place.

3   Improve the soil, if necessary, by incorporating ample organic matter. Soil preparation is not always necessary as long as drainage is good.

4   With a spade or trowel, dig holes the appropriate depth for your bulb type. Consult packaging, catalogues or a book on bulbs for planting depth. A depth of two to three times the length of the bulb is a good rule of thumb.

5   Add bone meal to the bottom of the hole and roughly mix it into the soil.

6   Place the bulb in the hole. Make sure you have the right side up (usually point up, roots down). The bottom of the bulb should rest firmly on the bottom of the hole

7   Refill the planting hole, tamping the soil lightly and water thoroughly.

✻ Tips

Many spring-flowering bulbs can be planted under deciduous trees. They will bloom before the tree comes into leaf and shades the planting area.

There are many tools to help you when planting a lot of bulbs. Some make perfect holes by removing small cylinders of soil.

Alternatively, dig a long trench instead of individual holes.

Things You'll Need

☐ spring-flowering bulbs ☐ spade or trowel ☐ bone meal

55 | Do Basic Winter Pruning

Deciduous trees and shrubs shed their leaves and go dormant over the winter. This is the perfect time to prune them without fear of interrupting their growth.

⊙ Steps

1 Remove any growth that comes from below the graft (where the top of the plant was originally joined to rootstock). Cut the growth as close to the main body of the plant as possible.

2 Look for and remove any dead, diseased or injured wood. Branches that are different in colour from the main body of the plant are suspect. Injuries may look like splits or blisters. Diseases may show up as black patches along the branch.

3 Cut into the tip of a suspect branch to make sure that it is dead. If it is green on the inside, it is still alive. If the branch is brown on the inside, it is probably dead. Keep cutting back from the tip until you reach green wood.

4 Remove any branches that cross through the centre of the plant; this will improve air circulation and discourage fungal disease.

5 Cut out any competing leaders – the upright growing limbs that will eventually turn into the main trunk. Most trees should have only one main branch heading vertically; multiple leaders and then trunks sap the energy from a tree and weaken it over time.

6 Prune for shape and size. In the case of fruit trees, keep the branches low so that you can reach the fruit. Most maples look best with a rounded crown, and most roses should be pruned in a low goblet shape. Know the basic shape of the plant you are working on.

7 Remove any water shoots from fruit trees. These are non-productive and light in colour and grow straight up, whereas fruiting wood is crooked and dark.

8 Rake up and remove all prunings and fallen leaves. Insects overwinter in fallen plant debris.

✱ Tip

Sharpen and oil your pruning tools before you start cutting.

⚠ Warning

Once the plants begin to grow leaves, sap is flowing through the branches. If you prune then, you take the chance of causing excessive bleeding.

Things You'll Need

☐ secateurs ☐ loppers ☐ long-handled loppers ☐ rake

56 | Plant a Bare-Root Tree or Shrub

Many kinds of shrubs and trees are sold while leafless and dormant, with roots bare of soil. A bare-root plant may look pathetic, but if you start it off properly and care for it well, it will thrive.

⊙ Steps

1   Plant bare-root trees and shrubs in late autumn, winter or early spring (from mid-November to April in most parts of the country) when the plants are dormant and the ground isn't frozen solid. They'll have a chance to put out new roots before they have to cope with hot sun, drying winds and the added stress of producing leaves.

2   Remove any packing material carefully, and rinse off or gently pull off any clumps of earth clinging to the roots; trim off any dead or damaged roots.

3   Immerse the roots in a bucket of water to soak for at least one to four hours, but no longer than overnight. Supplying enough moisture is key to the success of bare-root planting.

4   Dig a hole that's at least 60 cm (24 in) wider than the root system and about as deep as the point where the roots flare from the trunk (or stems in the case of a shrub). Using your spade, loosen the soil on the sides of the hole so it doesn't solidify around the plant's roots.

5   Mound soil in the bottom of the hole so that the peak reaches just about ground level.

6   Place stakes in the hole if you're planting a tree that will need support.

7   Set the tree or shrub on top of the mound so the roots cascade down over the sides. Spread them gently with your hands if you need to, and add or remove soil so that the crown of the root system is just at the surface of the ground. Use the soil mark on the plant as a guide to the correct planting depth.

8   Fill the hole about halfway with soil and tamp it lightly with your foot to remove large air pockets.

9   Make sure the tree or shrub is standing straight up, then water slowly to saturate the soil and remove any remaining air pockets.

10 Finish filling the hole with soil and water again.

11 Keep the soil moist for the first year after planting. Mulch to retain moisture, but keep at least 15 cm (6 in) bare around the trunk. Check frequently; if you see yellow leaves or the soil feels dry, water immediately.

✱ Tips

Unless you're planting a small shrub or a tree in a confined space, avoid improving the soil in the planting hole. The "good" soil will encourage the roots to confine themselves within that small area rather than spread out as they need to.

Deep, thorough watering is the key to healthy shrubs and trees. Give new trees at least 2.5 cm (1 in) of water a week all around the root zone. (The roots of a woody plant extend about the same distance as its branches.)

⚠ Warning

Use the bare-root method only for deciduous trees and shrubs of the standard size sold in nurseries. Larger deciduous plants and all evergreens will suffer too much stress without an extra cushion of soil around their roots.

Things You'll Need

☐ secateurs ☐ bucket ☐ spade ☐ stakes (optional) ☐ mulch

A root-balled tree or shrub comes with a hessian- or netting-wrapped clump of soil around its roots. Many evergreens are traditionally sold this way.

⊙ Steps

1 Buy root-balled trees or shrubs for planting in autumn or spring. Plants can also be set out during mild spells in winter if soil conditions allow.

2 Keep your tree or shrub in a cool, shady place until planting, cover the rootball with mulch, and keep the roots moist.

3 Calculate your hole dimensions carefully: A root-balled plant is heavy, but the roots are easily damaged. The less you have to move it, the better. You'll want to set the plant into the hole so that the bottom of the trunk (or trunks) is just above the soil surface.

4 Measure the rootball, then dig a hole about 15 cm (6 in) wider all around and roughly as deep. Lay a cane across the hole, measure the distance from the cane to the bottom of the hole and adjust the depth as needed.

5 Loosen the sides of the hole with your spade, and if your plant is too large to lift and lower without strain, cut down one side of the hole so that it forms a slope. You'll be able to simply slide the plant down the ramp and into the hole. Place stakes in the hole if you're planting a tree that will need support.

6 Move the plant to the hole very carefully. Ease the plant onto a plastic sheet and drag it to the site; don't roll it. If your plant is large, or if you have several, it pays to rent a special plant-moving trolley from a nursery or hire shop.

7 Lower the rootball into the hole, covering and all. Remove any synthetic wrappings or fastenings. Leave natural hessian and twine in place (they'll rot quickly), but cut away any hessian around the trunk; if it sticks out above ground it will wick moisture away from the roots.

8 Fill the hole about half way with soil and tamp it lightly with your foot to remove large air pockets. Make sure the tree or shrub is standing straight then water slowly to saturate the soil and remove any remaining air pockets.

9 Finish filling the hole with soil. Use any extra to build a temporary ridge at the drip line (the place on the ground directly below the outer edges of the foliage) and water again.

10 Keep the soil moist for the first year after planting. Mulch to retain moisture, but keep at least 15 cm (6 in) bare around the trunk. Check frequently; if you see yellow leaves or the soil feels dry, water immediately.

✱ Tips

Unless you're planting a small shrub or tree in a confined space, avoid improving the soil in the planting hole. The "good" soil will encourage the roots to confine themselves within that small area rather than spread out as they need to.

Deep, thorough watering is the key to healthy shrubs and trees. Give new trees at least 2.5 cm (1 in) of water a week all around the root zone. (The roots of a woody plant extend about the same distance as its branches.)

⚠ Warning

Even small root-balled shrubs are heavy. Unless you're dealing with tiny specimens, don't risk your back or the plant's roots and limbs – get help at planting time.

Things You'll Need

☐ spade ☐ bamboo cane ☐ plastic sheet ☐ mulch

Plant a Tree or Shrub From a Container   58

Many common nursery plants are sold in containers of various sizes and materials. Unlike bare-root and root-balled, container-grown plants can be planted even while growing vigorously.

⊙ Steps

1 Plant a container-grown tree or shrub in spring or autumn for the best results, especially if it's an evergreen. If that timing is not possible, though, any time except midsummer will work, as long as the soil is not bone-dry, saturated or frozen.

2 Dig a hole at least 15 cm (6 in) wider than the container and about the same depth. Then roughen up the sides of the hole with your spade.

3 Remove the plant from its container even if the label says you don't need to; the roots will spread out more quickly. With a small tree or shrub, it's easy to do this job before you lower the plant into its hole; with a larger plant, it's easier to handle if you place it into the hole first and then cut away the container.

4 Knock a plant out of a rigid plastic container. Simply tilt the pot onto its side, tap it lightly, and gently slide out the rootball. If the container is made of a soft material such as peat, cut the pot away using a knife or scissors.

5 Gently tease out any roots that are encircling the rootball with your fingers so that they are free, taking care not to break up the ball of soil. Then trim off any damaged roots.

6 Place a stake in the hole if you're planting a tree that will need support.

7 Set the plant into the hole at the same depth it was growing in the pot, and begin filling the hole, checking as you go to make sure the plant is standing up straight. Add about 10 cm (4 in) of soil and gently firm it with your foot or a hoe to remove any air pockets. Repeat the process until the hole is filled.

8 Water slowly to saturate the soil and remove any remaining air pockets.

9 Use any extra soil to build a temporary ridge at the drip line (the place on the ground directly below the outer edges of the foliage) and water again; the ridge will prevent the water from running off the soil.

10 Keep the soil moist for the first year after planting. Mulch to retain moisture, but keep at least 15 cm (6 in) bare around the trunk. Check frequently; if you see yellow leaves or the soil feels dry, water immediately.

✱ Tips

Unless you're planting a small shrub or tree in a confined space, avoid improving the soil in the planting hole. The "good" soil will encourage the roots to confine themselves within that small area rather than spread out as they need to.

Deep, thorough watering is the key to healthy shrubs and trees. Give new trees at least 2.5 cm (1 in) of water a week all around the root zone. (The roots of a woody plant extend about the same distance as its branches.)

When purchasing a tree or shrub in a container, make sure no roots are growing through the holes at the bottom of the container. The appearance of roots indicates that the plant is rootbound and may be under stress.

Things You'll Need

☐ spade ☐ mulch ☐ knife or scissors ☐ secateurs ☐ stake (optional)
☐ hoe

59 | Sow Seeds Indoors

Starting plants from seed indoors is a great way to get a head-start on spring. Although it takes a bit of a knack, it's not hard – especially when you know a few tricks of the trade.

⊙ Steps

1 Consider your timing. Some plants need to be planted as much as 12 weeks before your region's last average frost date, while others do best when started just two weeks before.

2 Choose your seed-sowing container. Nearly any container with drainage will do, but good candidates include milk carton bottoms, egg cartons, plastic produce boxes, peat pots, special seed-starting trays and modules divided into individual sections. (Punch drainage holes into containers that need them.)

3 Plant seeds in sterile seed compost. It has no soil to cause disease problems and is lightweight – perfect for baby plants to get off to a good start. Sprinkle vermiculite over seeds that require covering. Its lighter colour helps you see just what you've covered.

4 Follow seed packet directions about the depth of planting. As a rough rule, the larger the seed, the deeper it's planted. Some very small seeds are just scattered directly on the soil and not covered up at all.

5 Water gently. Either set the container in 2.5–5 cm (1–2 in) of warm water and allow the water to wick up to the soil surface, water gently from above with a fine-rose watering can, or dribble water from your hand.

6 Slip the container into a clear plastic bag to minimise draughts and conserve moisture. Twist the end shut.

7 Put the seeds in a spot at the correct temperature. (Check the seed packet.) Keep the seeds out of direct sunlight or risk fatally overheating them. Seeds usually need either cool temperatures of 10–18°C (50–65°F) or warm temperatures of 21–30°C (70–85°F). Find the right spot by checking with a thermometer in different locations in your house.

8 Check the seeds daily. If water drops form inside the bag, open the end to air it. Once the seeds germinate, remove the plastic and put the seedlings in the brightest indoor spot possible.

9   Put the new seedlings in a sunny, unobstructed south-facing window.

✱ Tips

If you've planted the seedlings more than a couple of weeks before the
last frost date, it's a good idea to prick them out, transplanting them into
individual pots so that they have plenty of room to grow. To do this, lift the
seedlings out gently with a kitchen knife and plant them in regular potting
soil.

Things You'll Need

☐ seeds ☐ containers ☐ seed compost ☐ vermiculite ☐ clear plastic bag

Sow Seeds Outdoors   60

Whether you're planting flowers, vegetables or herbs, sowing
seeds outdoors is simple. All it takes is good garden soil and a
little follow-up care to get loads of great plants.

⊙ Steps

1   Read seed-packet directions carefully. Many annuals and perennials can
    be sown directly in the ground, but some should be started in containers,
    then transplanted.

2   Consider your timing. Some plants like to be planted outdoors in early
    spring, while temperatures are cold. Others must wait until after your area's
    average last frost date. Again, consult the packet.

3   Prepare the soil. Most seeds demand optimum conditions. Work in plenty
    of compost with a spade or fork to a depth of at least 30 cm (12 in). The
    soil should be loose and crumbly and moist before planting. Rake smooth.

4   Sow the seed. Follow packet directions on sowing depth. As a rough rule,
    the larger the seed, the deeper it must be planted. Some very small seeds
    are just scattered directly on the soil and not covered up at all.

5   Water gently. It's easy for seeds to be washed away by heavy watering.
    Mist the soil gently with a water sprayer or use a watering can that has a
    gentle sprinkle. Be sure to keep soil moist until seedlings emerge.

6   Thin out seedlings by gently pulling them out, if the seed packet directs,
    once they are 2.5 cm (1 in) or so high. This will ensure that those you want
    to survive have adequate room to grow big and healthy.

7   Pinch out most seedlings when they've made three sets of true leaves.
    Just take the top part of the tiny plant off with your fingernails to
    encourage bushy growth and more roots. Check the packet first to
    determine whether pinching is recommended.

8   Look after your seedlings. Make sure they continue to have all the sun they
    need. Also keep the seedlings watered and weeded. Add up to 5 cm (2 in)
    of organic mulch as soon as seedlings are up and growing.

✱ Tips

Some plants are easier than others to start from seed: marigolds, zinnias and
nasturtiums are easy-to-start examples.

It's better to trim crowded seedlings off at soil level than to disturb the ones you want to keep by pulling the crowding ones out by the roots.

Things You'll Need

☐ seeds ☐ spade or fork ☐ rake ☐ watering can or water sprayer ☐ mulch

---

61	Transplant Seedlings

Whether you grow your fledgling plants from seed or buy them at the nursery, extra care at planting time will get them off to a good start in your garden.

⊙ Steps

1 Double-check the planting date on the seed packet, in a comprehensive garden book or on the plastic tag stuck into the soil (for plants you bought at a nursery). You must hold off planting most flowers and vegetables until all danger of frost has passed. Some cold-tolerant varieties such as cauliflower can go into the ground a bit earlier; heat lovers such as tomatoes should wait until the ground has thoroughly warmed up.

2 Prepare the planting bed. Use a spade or fork to work the soil to a depth of 25–30 cm (10–12 in); incorporate organic matter as needed.

3 "Harden off" your seedlings by leaving them outdoors for longer and longer periods. Start by sheltering the young plants under a porch or bench by day, then bringing them back in by night or during inclement weather. After two or three days, you can safely keep them in the sun for half a day. By the end of a week, they'll be tough enough to soak up the rays all day.

4 If you can, transplant the seedlings to the garden on an overcast day to ease the shock of transition from pot to ground. If a light drizzle is falling, so much the better. Water both the ground outside and the plants before you move them into the garden.

5 Remove each plant from its pot by turning it upside down and tapping lightly on the bottom; it will slide out easily. Gently run your fingers through the roots to loosen them a little.

6 Use a trowel to dig a hole about twice the size of the rootball and set the plant into the hole so the rootball will be covered by about 5mm of soil. Press the soil firmly around the roots to ensure good soil-to-root contact.

7 Space the plants according to the directions on the packet.

8 Water well immediately after transplanting and again every day until the plants are well established and growing – usually within a week. If some plants show signs of wilting, shield them with a piece of lattice until they perk up, which shouldn't take more than a few days.

✱ Tip

If the plant has been growing in a peat pot, break away a few pieces from the bottom or sides so the roots won't be confined, and loosen the soil a little with your fingers.

⚠ Warning

If you live where late frosts can hit unexpectedly, be prepared to protect your tender seedlings. When the weather forecast predicts low temperatures, cover them with Styrofoam cups, plastic bottles cut in half or one of several commercial products made for the purpose. Or invest in some cloches. Traditional beautiful, bell-shaped glass covers have been used for centuries to shield tender plants from sudden cold, or simply to prolong the growing season.

Things You'll Need

☐ seedlings ☐ spade or fork ☐ organic matter ☐ garden trowel
☐ watering can or garden hose

Design and Prepare a Flower Bed 　　62

A well-prepared flower bed not only looks good but promotes good drainage, has plenty of nutrients, makes watering and weeding easy, and discourages disease and pests.

⊙ Steps

1 Choose a spot for the bed and walk around it. Visualise plants of different shapes and sizes. Consider their needs for sun and shade. Make rough sketches.

2 Sketch a plan of the bed you want to plant. Tall plants should go at the back of a bed that's adjacent to a wall or fence and in the middle of a bed that will be viewed from all sides. Plants that need frequent attention, such as pruning, deadheading or spraying, should go where they can be reached without your crushing other plants.

3 Sprinkle flour or sand to trace the outline of your prospective flower bed. If you don't like the way it looks, brush it away and start again.

4 Use a trowel or small spade and cut along the lines you've just marked out, then remove the grass from the surface.

5 Have your soil tested, or test it yourself with a home kit, and improve it as necessary. A local nursery can recommend the best products to use.

6 To eliminate weeds, dig over the area. Then leave it for at least a week to allow annual weed seeds in the soil to germinate. Hoe or dig it a second time to remove the weeds. Alternatively, spray the area with a non-selective herbicide, following directions carefully, especially regarding how long to wait until planting.

7 Spread 8–10 cm (3–4 in) of compost and any other fertilisers over the top of the area you intend for the bed.

8 Till or dig up the soil to a depth of at least 20–25 cm (8–10 in), up to 60 cm (24 in) if you're planting perennials.

9 Toss out any large stones that appear on the surface.

10 Rake the surface smooth, and you are ready to plant.

11 Add edging, if desired. Edging isn't a must but does help keep out grass and some other weeds while creating a neat appearance.

✱ Tips

There's no need to limit your bed to a rectangular shape. Flower beds can be any size or shape you wish.

Unless you've got a budget big enough to buy full-grown perennials, the plants you put in the ground now will look very different in a year or two. Leave room for them to grow. You can fill in bare spots with annuals.

⚠ Warning

This method for creating a new flower bed works only if the soil is reasonably good. In areas with very sandy or very heavy clay soil, raised beds are your best bet. Or if you don't mind the work, dig out and dispose of the problem soil, and replace it with a mixture of compost and high-quality topsoil.

Things You'll Need

☐ flour or sand ☐ trowel ☐ compost ☐ hoe or spade ☐ rake

63 Plant a Garden Bed

After you've prepared the soil and raked it smooth, the next step is to add the plants. Here's what to do.

⊙ Steps

1 Remove seedlings from their containers, and loosen the roots gently if they're root-bound. Place the unpotted plants back into the nursery tray, lying on their sides with the foliage all facing the same direction. Work quickly so the roots don't dry out.

2 Begin planting at the back of the garden bed. This way you won't be stepping all over the plants you've just put into the ground. Keep the tray of plants where you can easily reach it.

3 Use a trowel to make a hole for each plant. Stab the trowel into the soil, trying to gauge the depth so that the hole is only as deep as the rootball. The crown (the area where the foliage meets the rootball) of the plant should be at the surface of the soil.

4 Pick up the rootball of a plant with your free hand.

5 Lower the plant into the prepared hole.

6 Adjust the depth if necessary. With your trowel, shovel in a little soil to fill the hole around the plant, or scoop out a little more soil to make room for the plant. You want the top of the rootball to be at the surface of the soil.

7 Push the soil into place around the roots with your trowel.

8 Continue working backwards, planting as you work toward the front of the bed.

9 Cover your footsteps by roughing up the soil with your trowel. Tender young roots push through soft, uncompacted soil much faster than through compacted soil.

10 Water the newly planted garden immediately after you've finished planting the entire bed. Use a hose at low volume or a watering can. Try not to get water on the foliage; apply it near the roots to settle the soil.

✳ Tips

Plant in the early morning or late afternoon to prevent roots from drying out.

Avoid using fertiliser until you begin to see new growth.

Stand up and stretch your back every 15 minutes while planting.

Things You'll Need

☐ seedlings ☐ garden trowel ☐ garden hose or watering can

Grow Popular Vegetables | 64

Home-grown produce almost always tastes better than shop-bought. Look for seeds and seedlings in nurseries and catalogues and on websites, and choose with an awareness of what will grow best in your region and climate.

Carrots

- Choose a site in full sun. Dig at least 30cm (12 in) deep, and remove all rocks and debris. Add plenty of organic matter.
- Sow directly in the ground from about two to three weeks before the last expected frost.
- Thin seedlings before tops entwine. Pinch out the leaves to thin – pulling the carrots whole attracts carrot fly. Mulch with compost.
- Water in dry spells and when plants are young, but do not overwater; cut back on watering as they near maturity
- Begin harvesting when roots have turned bright orange.

Courgettes

- Choose a site with full sun. Courgettes need soil that's rich, moisture-retentive and well-draining. Dig in plenty of compost and well-rotted manure.
- Sow seed indoors in mid- to late spring or outdoors in early summer. Plant out home-grown or bought plants in early summer when frosts are over.
- Feed if plants appear to be growing slowly. Train trailing courgettes over wires.
- Water regularly, especially during flowering.
- Harvest when the flowers fall off or when the courgettes are about 10 cm (4 in) long If left longer, flavour deteriorates.

Lettuce

- Plant in full sun or in light shade in midsummer. Dig the soil thoroughly, breaking up clumps and removing stones and debris. Work in plenty of compost and well-rotted manure.
- Sow seeds outdoors as soon as the soil can be worked in spring. Keep sowing through the season for continuous crops Plant bought lettuce plants 15–25 cm (6–10 in) apart.
- Feed occasionally with liquid fertiliser if growth seems slow.
- Keep the soil moist, especially in dry weather, but avoid watering in the evening; foliage that stays wet overnight is prone to disease.
- Begin cutting leaf lettuces as soon as they're big enough to use. Harvest heading types when heads are firm and fully formed.

Peas

- Choose a site with full sun and well-draining soil. Dig in plenty of compost. Avoid any high-nitrogen soil additives.

- Sow directly outdoors as soon as soil can be worked. Plant 2.5 cm (1 in) deep, 8–10 cm (3–4 in) apart, in rows 90 cm (3 ft) apart. Install supports.
- Help ensure heavy yields by using liquid fertiliser twice during growing season. Guide climbing types upwards as soon as they're long enough to climb.
- Give young plants about 1 cm (½ in) of water a week (twice that in very sandy soil). When plants begin to flower, give them 2.5 cm (1 in) per week.
- Expect peas to be ready for picking about three weeks after the plants begin to flower.

Potatoes

- Choose an open, sunny site. Work in plenty of well-rotted manure the autumn before planting and add a fetiliser.
- Prepare tubers by "chitting" them: put them in trays in a cool, light place until they produce short green shoots. Plant the potatoes in holes or trenches 30–38 cm (12–15 in) deep.
- Earth up potatoes as they grow, piling soil around the stems to ensure the potatoes do not come to the soil surface.
- Water well to keep the plants and tubers moist but not waterlogged.
- Harvest early potatoes when the plant flowers. Leave maincrop potatoes longer to increase in size.

Tomatoes

- Tomatoes need full sun and plenty of warmth. Improve the soil with compost.
- Move seedlings to the garden when they have their first flower buds and all danger of frost is past. Dig a hole the size of a football for each plant. Mix in a spade of compost. Set plants 38–45 cm (15–18 in) apart.
- Mulch soil and install any supports the plants will need as they grow. Feed with low-nitrogen fertiliser: after the first flowers appear, when fruits are as big as golf balls, and when you spot the first ripe tomato.
- Keep plants continually moist, especially during dry spells. Erratic watering results in poor fruits.
- Pick tomatoes when their colour is glossy and even, and their texture is midway between soft and firm. Pick green tomatoes at the end of the season and leave in a warm place to ripen.

65 | Protect Your Garden From Slugs and Snails

There's no sure way to get rid of slugs and snails in your garden. All you can do is be vigilant and try to discourage them. Here are some ways to keep slugs and snails off your plants.

⊙ Steps

1 Be aware of what slugs and snails like best – seedlings, small annuals, climbers, herbaceous perennials and vegetables. Try planting seedlings out at a later stage when their leaves are less appealing to slugs, or grow particularly precious plants in pots, where they are less likely to suffer.

2 Dig over the soil regularly to expose slug and snail eggs so that birds will eat them.

3 Clear away fallen leaves and other debris under which slugs and snails hide during the day.

4 Water on some nematodes; these are minute parasites that attack and kill slugs. You can buy them by mail order and they should be applied between March and October when the temperature is 5–20°C (41–68°F). Each set of nematodes is effective for up to six weeks.

5 Spread grit or broken shells or eggshells as a mulch around plants prone to attack. Slugs and snails dislike the rough surface.

6 Set traps. Put out halves of grapefruit or melon peel in the evening, open side down – the slugs and snails will crawl in attracted by the smell and you can collect them and dispose of them in the morning. Alternatively, sink a container half-filled with beer or milk into the soil, leaving 2–3 cm (1 in) of rim above ground. The slugs and snails will crawl in and drown, while beneficial ground beetles will stay out.

7 Make a ring of copper tape around precious plants or pots. The copper strips emit an electrical charge when in contact with slug and snail slime.

8 Go out at night with a torch and collect the slugs and snails by hand.

9 Apply slug pellets and liquids. Aluminium sulphate-based products are least harmful to other wildlife.

❋ Tip

A nighttime patrol is even more effective after rain, when slugs and snails particularly like to feed.

⚠ Warning

Slug pellets can harm cats, dogs and birds that eat the poisoned slugs. Use them as a last resort, and if there are pets in the garden, put the pellets in a tube beside vulnerable plants so that the dead slugs and snails are less visible and so less likely to be eaten.

Deadhead Flowers	66

A flowering plant's goal is to set seed. If you repeatedly deadhead – trim off the spent flowers – the plant goes into overdrive, putting out more and more flowers in an effort to reproduce.

◉ Steps

1 Deadhead when a flower starts to brown, wither, shatter or otherwise deteriorate.

2 Deadhead tall flowers that sit on long, slender stems by cutting the stem at the base of the plant.

3 Trim bushy plants with many small flowers with handheld shears or small hedge clippers. Trim the whole plant at once – even if there are still some nice flowers left – rather than trying to tediously trim one flower at a time.

4 Deadhead other plants by simply snapping or pinching off the flowers with your hand or cut them off with shears, a knife or scissors.

5 Treat annuals and perennials that have dying or ragged foliage by cutting back (shortening) the foliage by one-third to two-thirds. Do this either when

the plant has stopped blooming or when it starts to get that overall tatty look. It will usually send out a new flush of healthy, fresh foliage with flowers.

✳ Tip

Plants respond differently to deadheading, depending on climate, variety, rainfall and other variables. Experiment. Take comfort in the fact that in most cases, the worst you can do is give them a bad haircut. It's almost impossible to kill a plant by deadheading.

Things You'll Need

❑ secateurs, shears or small hedge clippers

---

67 | Train a Climber

Climbers are quick-change artists that can hide garden eyesores. There are four basic types of climber, each growing in a different way.

◉ Steps

1 Plant climbers such as ivy or climbing hydrangea at the base of any wall or fence you want to cover. Stand back and watch them scramble upwards. They will send out rootlets that will cling to any support they encounter.

2 Plant climbers with tendrils such as grapes and sweet peas where they can hang on to their supports. Their tendrils grow out from their stems and can wrap themselves around thin supports such as string, wire or the stems of other plants. Match the support to the size and weight of the mature plant; a grapevine needs a sturdy support with strong wires, while sweet peas need only a simple wire or nylon mesh trellis.

3 Plant twining climbers such as clematis and morning glory near any trellis, arbour or openwork fence. As the plants grow, they'll twine themselves around both vertical and horizontal supports. Guide the first shoots up the fence and fasten them loosely; once they start weaving their way through the openings, they will need no more help.

4 Fasten climbers with no means of self-support, such as jasmine, directly to a fence or trellis. Secure the shoots loosely using plastic-coated wire or nylon twine tied in a figure-of-eight. To cover a wall or solid fence, drive in galvanised nails at 45–60 cm (18–24 in) intervals, and as the shoots grow, tie them to the nails.

✳ Tips

Look to the future if you plant a perennial climber. Wisteria, for instance, will live 50 years or more, and a mature plant is heavy. It needs a sturdy, well-designed structure that will both show off its beauty and bear its weight.

Arrange the shoots of tendril climbers in the direction you want them to grow, and fasten them loosely with twine or coated twist ties for a day or so until the tendrils begin to grip.

Things You'll Need

❑ twine or other ties ❑ trellis ❑ galvanised nails